Kansas City Royals 2021

A Baseball Companion

Edited by Steven Goldman and Bret Sayre

Baseball Prospectus

Craig Brown, Associate Editor
Robert Au, Harry Pavlidis and Amy Pircher, Statistics Editors

Copyright © 2021 by DIY Baseball, LLC.
All rights reserved

This book or any part thereof may not be reproduced or transmitted in any form or by any means, electronic or mechanical, including photocopying, recording, or by any information storage and retrieval system, without permission in writing from the publisher.

Limit of Liability/Disclaimer of Warranty: While the publisher and the author have used their best efforts in preparing this book, they make no representations or warranties with respect to the accuracy or completeness of the contents of this book and specifically disclaim any implied warranties of merchantability or fitness for a particular purpose. No warranty may be created or extended by sales representatives or written sales materials. The advice and strategies contained herein may not be suitable for your situation. You should consult with a professional where appropriate. Neither the publisher nor the author shall be liable for any loss of profit or any other commercial damages, including but not limited to special, incidental, consequential, or other damages.

Library of Congress Cataloging-in-Publication Data:
paperback
ISBN-13: 978-1-950716-47-0

Project Credits
Cover Design: Ginny Searle
Interior Design and Production: Amy Pircher, Robert Au
Layout: Amy Pircher, Robert Au

Baseball icon courtesy of Uberux, from https://www.shareicon.net/author/uberux

Ballpark diagram courtesy of Lou Spirito/THIRTY81 Project, https://thirty81project.com/

Manufactured in the United States of America
10 9 8 7 6 5 4 3 2 1

Table of Contents

Statistical Introduction v

Part 1: Team Analysis

Performance Graphs 3
2020 Team Performance 4
2021 Team Projections 5
Team Personnel 6
Kauffman Stadium Stats 7
Royals Team Analysis 9

Part 2: Player Analysis

Royals Player Analysis 16
Royals Prospects 89

Part 3: Featured Articles

Royals All-Time Top 10 Players 103
    by Rob Mains

A Taxonomy of 2020 Abnormalities 109
    by Rob Mains

Tranches of WAR 115
    by Russell A. Carleton

Secondhand Sport 121
    by Patrick Dubuque

Steve Dalkowski Dreaming 125
    by Steven Goldman

A Reward For A Functioning Society 129
    by Cory Frontin and Craig Goldstein

Index of Names 133

Statistical Introduction

Sports are, fundamentally, a blend of athletic endeavor and storytelling. Baseball, like any other sport, tells its stories in so many ways: in the arc of a game from the stands or a season from the box scores, in photos, or even in numbers. At Baseball Prospectus, we understand that statistics don't replace observation or any of baseball's stories, but complement everything else that makes the game so much fun.

What stats help us with is with patterns and precision, variance and value. This book can help you learn things you may not see from watching a game or hundred, whether it's the path of a career over time or the breadth of the entire MLB. We'd also never ask you to choose between our numbers and the experience of viewing a game from the cheap seats or the comfort of your home; our publication combines running the numbers with observations and wisdom from some of the brightest minds we can find. But if you *do* want to learn more about the numbers beyond what's on the backs of player jerseys, let us help explain.

Offense

We've revised our methodology for determining batting value. Long-time readers of the book will notice that we've retired True Average in favor of a new metric: Deserved Runs Created Plus (DRC+). Developed by Jonathan Judge and our stats team, this statistic measures everything a player does at the plate–reaching base, hitting for power, making outs, and moving runners over–and puts it on a scale where 100 equals league-average performance. A DRC+ of 150 is terrific, a DRC+ of 100 is average and a DRC+ of 75 means you better be an excellent defender.

DRC+ also does a better job than any of our previous metrics in taking contextual factors into account. The model adjusts for how the park affects performance, but also for things like the talent of the opposing pitcher, value of different types of batted-ball events, league, temperature and other factors. It's able to describe a player's expected offensive contribution than any other statistic we've found over the years, and also does a better job of predicting future performance as well.

The other aspect of run-scoring is baserunning, which we quantify using Baserunning Runs. BRR not only records the value of stolen bases (or getting caught in the act), but also accounts for all the stuff that doesn't show up on the back of a baseball card: a runner's ability to go first to third on a single, or advance on a fly ball.

Defense

Where offensive value is *relatively* easy to identify and understand, defensive value is ... not. Over the past dozen years, the sabermetric community has focused mostly on stats based on zone data: a real-live human person records the type of batted ball and estimated landing location, and models are created that give expected outs. From there, you can compare fielders' actual outs to those expected ones. Simple, right?

Unfortunately, zone data has two major issues. First, zone data is recorded by commercial data providers who keep the raw data private unless you pay for it. (All the statistics we build in this book and on our website use public data as inputs.) That hurts our ability to test assumptions or duplicate results. Second, over the years it has become apparent that there's quite a bit of "noise" in zone-based fielding analysis. Sometimes the conclusions drawn from zone data don't hold up to scrutiny, and sometimes the different data provided by different providers don't look anything alike, giving wildly different results. Sometimes the hard-working professional stringers or scorers might unknowingly inflict unconscious bias into the mix: for example good fielders will often be credited with more expected outs despite the data, and ballparks with high press boxes tend to score more line drives than ones with a lower press box.

Enter our Fielding Runs Above Average (FRAA). For most positions, FRAA is built from play-by-play data, which allows us to avoid the subjectivity found in many other fielding metrics. The idea is this: count how many fielding plays are made by a given player and compare that to expected plays for an average fielder at their position (based on pitcher ground ball tendencies and batter handedness). Then we adjust for park and base-out situations.

When it comes to catchers, our methodology is a little different thanks to the laundry list of responsibilities they're tasked with beyond just, well, catching and throwing the ball. By now you've probably heard about "framing" or the art of making umpires more likely to call balls outside the strike zone for strikes. To put this into one tidy number, we incorporate pitch tracking data (for the years it exists) and adjust for important factors like pitcher, umpire, batter and home-field advantage using a mixed-model approach. This grants us a number for how many strikes the catcher is personally adding to (or subtracting from) his pitchers' performance ... which we then convert to runs added or lost using linear weights.

Framing is one of the biggest parts of determining catcher value, but we also take into account blocking balls from going past, whether a scorer deems it a passed ball or a wild pitch. We use a similar approach—one that really benefits from the pitch tracking data that tells us what ends up in the dirt and what doesn't. We also include a catcher's ability to prevent stolen bases and how well they field balls in play, and *finally* we come up with our FRAA for catchers.

Pitching

Both pitching and fielding make up the half of baseball that isn't run scoring: run prevention. Separating pitching from fielding is a tough task, and most recent pitching analysis has branched off from Voros McCracken's famous (and controversial) statement, "There is little if any difference among major-league pitchers in their ability to prevent hits on balls hit in the field of play." The research of the analytic community has validated this to some extent, and there are a host of "defense-independent" pitching measures that have been developed to try and extract the effect of the defense behind a hurler from the pitcher's work.

Our solution to this quandary is Deserved Run Average (DRA), our core pitching metric. DRA seeks to evaluate a pitcher's performance, much like earned run average (ERA), the tried-and-true pitching stat you've seen on every baseball broadcast or box score from the past century, but it's very different. To start, DRA takes an event-by-event look at what the pitchers does, and adjusts the value of that event based on different environmental factors like park, batter, catcher, umpire, base-out situation, run differential, inning, defense, home field advantage, pitcher role and temperature. That mixed model gives us a pitcher's expected contribution, similar to what we do for our DRC+ model for hitters and FRAA model for catchers. (Oh, and we also consider the pitcher's effect on basestealing and on balls getting past the catcher.)

DRA is set to the scale of runs allowed per nine innings (RA9) instead of ERA, which makes DRA's scale slightly higher than ERA's. Because of this, for ease of use, we're supplying DRA-, which is much easier for the reader to parse. As with DRC+, DRA- is an "index" stat, meaning instead of using some arbitrary and shifting number to denote what's "good," average is always 100. The reason that it uses a minus rather than a plus is because like ERA, a lower number is better. Therefore a 75 DRA- describes a performance 25 percent better than average, whereas a 150 DRA- means that either a pitcher is getting extremely lucky with their results, or getting ready to try a new pitch.

Since the last time you picked up an edition of this book, we've also made a few minor changes to DRA to make it better. Recent research into "tunneling"—the act of throwing consecutive pitches that appear similar from a batter's point of view until after the swing decision point–data has given us a new contextual factor to account for in DRA: plate distance. This refers to the distance between successive pitches as they approach the plate, and while it has a smaller effect than factors like velocity or whiff rate, it still can help explain pitcher strikeout rate in our model.

Recently Added Descriptive Statistics

Returning to our 2021 edition of the book are a few figures which recently appeared. These numbers may be a little bit more familiar to those of you who have spent some time investigating baseball statistics.

Fastball Percentage

Our fastball percentage (FA%) statistic measures how frequently a pitcher throws a pitch classified as a "fastball," measured as a percentage of overall pitches thrown. We qualify three types of fastballs:

1. The traditional four-seam fastball;
2. The two-seam fastball or sinker;
3. "Hard cutters," which are pitches that have the movement profile of a cut fastball and are used as the pitcher's primary offering or in place of a more traditional fastball.

For example, a pitcher with a FA% of 67 throws any combination of these three pitches about two-thirds of the time.

Whiff Rate

Everybody loves a swing and a miss, and whiff rate (Whiff%) measures how frequently pitchers induce a swinging strike. To calculate Whiff%, we add up all the pitches thrown that ended with a swinging strike, then divide that number by a pitcher's total pitches thrown. Most often, high whiff rates correlate with high strikeout rates (and overall effective pitcher performance).

Called Strike Probability

Called Strike Probability (CSP) is a number that represents the likelihood that all of a pitcher's pitches will be called a strike while controlling for location, pitcher and batter handedness, umpire and count. Here's how it works: on each pitch, our model determines how many times (out of 100) that a similar pitch was called for a strike given those factors mentioned above, and when normalized for each batter's strike zone. Then we average the CSP for all pitches thrown by a pitcher in a season, and that gives us the yearly CSP percentage you see in the stats boxes.

As you might imagine, pitchers with a higher CSP are more likely to work in the zone, where pitchers with a lower CSP are likely locating their pitches outside the normal strike zone, for better or for worse.

Projections

Many of you aren't turning to this book just for a look at what a player has done, but for a look at what a player is going to do: the PECOTA projections. PECOTA, initially developed by Nate Silver (who has moved on to greater fame as a political analyst), consists of three parts:

1. Major-league equivalencies, which use minor-league statistics to project how a player will perform in the major leagues;
2. Baseline forecasts, which use weighted averages and regression to the mean to estimate a player's current true talent level; and
3. Aging curves, which uses the career paths of comparable players to estimate how a player's statistics are likely to change over time.

With all those important things covered, let's take a look at what's in the book this year.

Team Prospectus

Most of this book is composed of team chapters, with one for each of the 30 major-league franchises. On the first page of each chapter, you'll see a box that contains some of the key statistics for each team as well as a very inviting stadium diagram.

We start with the team name, their unadjusted 2020 win-loss record, and their divisional ranking. Beneath that are a host of other team statistics. **Pythag** presents an adjusted 2020 winning percentage, calculated by taking runs scored per game (**RS/G**) and runs allowed per game (**RA/G**) for the team, and running them through a version of Bill James' Pythagorean formula that was refined and improved by David Smyth and Brandon Heipp. (The formula is called "Pythagenpat," which is equally fun to type and to say.)

Next up is **DRC+**, described earlier, to indicate the overall hitting ability of the team either above or below league-average. Run prevention on the pitching side is covered by **DRA** (also mentioned earlier) and another metric: Fielding Independent Pitching (**FIP**), which calculates another ERA-like statistic based on strikeouts, walks, and home runs recorded. Defensive Efficiency Rating (**DER**) tells us the percentage of balls in play turned into outs for the team, and is a quick fielding shorthand that rounds out run prevention.

After that, we have several measures related to roster composition, as opposed to on-field performance. **B-Age** and **P-Age** tell us the average age of a team's batters and pitchers, respectively. **Payroll** is the combined team payroll for all on-field players, and Doug Pappas' Marginal Dollars per Marginal Win (**M$/MW**) tells us how much money a team spent to earn production above replacement level.

Kansas City Royals 2021

Next to each of these stats, we've listed each team's MLB rank in that category from first to 30th. In this, first always indicates a positive outcome and 30th a negative outcome, except in the case of salary—first is highest.

After the franchise statistics, we share a few items about the team's home ballpark. There's the aforementioned diagram of the park's dimensions (including distances to the outfield wall), a graphic showing the height of the wall from the left-field pole to the right-field pole, and a table showing three-year park factors for the stadium. The park factors are displayed as indexes where 100 is average, 110 means that the park inflates the statistic in question by 10 percent, and 90 means that the park deflates the statistic in question by 10 percent.

On the second page of each team chapter, you'll find three graphs. The first is **Payroll History** and helps you see how the team's payroll has compared to the MLB and divisional average payrolls over time. Payroll figures are current as of January 1, 2021; with so many free agents still unsigned as of this writing, the final 2021 figure will likely be significantly different for many teams. (In the meantime, you can always find the most current data at Baseball Prospectus' Cot's Baseball Contracts page.)

The second graph is **Future Commitments** and helps you see the team's future outlays, if any.

The third graph is **Farm System Ranking** and displays how the Baseball Prospectus prospect team has ranked the organization's farm system since 2007.

After the graphs, we have a **Personnel** section that lists many of the important decision-makers and upper-level field and operations staff members for the franchise, as well as any former Baseball Prospectus staff members who are currently part of the organization. (In very rare circumstances, someone might be on both lists!)

Position Players

After all that information and a thoughtful bylined essay covering each team, we present our player comments. These are also bylined, but due to frequent franchise shifts during the offseason, our bylines are more a rough guide than a perfect accounting of who wrote what.

Each player is listed with the major-league team that employed him as of early January 2021. If a player changed teams after that point via free agency, trade, or any other method, you'll be able to find them in the chapter for their previous squad.

As an example, take a look at the player comment for Padres shortstop Fernando Tatis Jr.: the stat block that accompanies his written comment is at the top of this page. First we cover biographical information (age is as of June 30, 2021) before moving onto the stats themselves. Our statistic columns include standard identifying information like **YEAR**, **TEAM**, **LVL** (level of affiliated play) and **AGE** before getting into the numbers. Next, we provide raw, untranslated

Fernando Tatis Jr. SS

Born: 01/02/99 Age: 22 Bats: R Throws: R
Height: 6'3" Weight: 217 Origin: International Free Agent, 2015

YEAR	TEAM	LVL	AGE	PA	R	2B	3B	HR	RBI	BB	K	SB	CS	AVG/OBP/SLG
2018	SA	AA	19	394	77	22	4	16	43	33	109	16	5	.286/.355/.507
2019	SD	MLB	20	372	61	13	6	22	53	30	110	16	6	.317/.379/.590
2020	SD	MLB	21	257	50	11	2	17	45	27	61	11	3	.277/.366/.571
2021 FS	SD	MLB	22	600	95	24	4	31	81	50	165	17	8	.263/.331/.499
2021 DC	SD	MLB	22	628	100	25	4	32	85	53	173	19	8	.263/.331/.499

Comparables: Darryl Strawberry, Bo Bichette, Ronald Acuña Jr.

YEAR	TEAM	LVL	AGE	PA	DRC+	BABIP	BRR	FRAA	WARP
2018	SA	AA	19	394	136	.370	3.0	SS(83): -1.9	2.4
2019	SD	MLB	20	372	118	.410	7.1	SS(83): 0.9	3.4
2020	SD	MLB	21	257	126	.306	0.7	SS(57): -5.5	0.9
2021 FS	SD	MLB	22	600	126	.318	1.7	SS -1	3.9
2021 DC	SD	MLB	22	628	126	.318	1.8	SS -1	4.0

numbers like you might find on the back of your dad's baseball cards: **PA** (plate appearances), **R** (runs), **2B** (doubles), **3B** (triples), **HR** (home runs), **RBI** (runs batted in), **BB** (walks), **K** (strikeouts), **SB** (stolen bases) and **CS** (caught stealing).

Following the basic stats is **Whiff%** (whiff rate), which denotes how often, when a batter swings, he fails to make contact with the ball. Another way to think of this number is an inverse of a hitter's contact rate.

Next, we have unadjusted "slash" statistics: **AVG** (batting average), **OBP** (on-base percentage) and **SLG** (slugging percentage). Following the slash line is **DRC+** (Deserved Runs Created Plus), which we described earlier as total offensive expected contribution compared to the league average.

BABIP (batting average on balls in play) tells us how often a ball in play fell for a hit, and can help us identify whether a batter may have been lucky or not ... but note that high BABIPs also tend to follow the great hitters of our time, as well as speedy singles hitters who put the ball on the ground.

The next item is **BRR** (Baserunning Runs), which covers all of a player's baserunning accomplishments including (but not limited to) swiped bags and failed attempts. Next is **FRAA** (Fielding Runs Above Average), which also includes the number of games previously played at each position noted in parentheses. Multi-position players have only their two most frequent positions listed here, but their total FRAA number reflects all positions played.

Our last column here is **WARP** (Wins Above Replacement Player). WARP estimates the total value of a player, which means for hitters it takes into account hitting runs above average (calculated using the DRC+ model), BRR and FRAA. Then, it makes an adjustment for positions played and gives the player a credit for plate appearances based upon the difference between "replacement level"—which is derived from the quality of players added to a team's roster after the start of the season–and the league average.

The final line just below the stats box is **PECOTA** data, which is discussed further in a following section.

Catchers

Catchers are a special breed, and thus they have earned their own separate box which displays some of the defensive metrics that we've built just for them. As an example, let's check out Yasmani Grandal.

YEAR	TEAM	P. COUNT	FRM RUNS	BLK RUNS	THRW RUNS	TOT RUNS
2018	LAD	16816	15.7	0.8	0.1	16.5
2019	MIL	18740	19.4	1.8	-0.1	21.1
2020	CHW	4830	3.7	0.3	-0.2	3.8
2021	CHW	14430	16.7	-0.6	1.0	17.1
2021	CHW	14430	16.7	0.4	1.0	18.0

The **YEAR** and **TEAM** columns match what you'd find in the other stat box. **P. COUNT** indicates the number of pitches thrown while the catcher was behind the plate, including swinging strikes, fouls and balls in play. **FRM RUNS** is the total run value the catcher provided (or cost) his team by influencing the umpire to call strikes where other catchers did not. **BLK RUNS** expresses the total run value above or below average for the catcher's ability to prevent wild pitches and passed balls. **THRW RUNS** is calculated using a similar model as the previous two statistics, and it measures a catcher's ability to throw out basestealers but also to dissuade them from testing his arm in the first place. It takes into account factors like the pitcher (including his delivery and pickoff move) and baserunner (who could be as fast as Billy Hamilton or as slow as Yonder Alonso). **TOT RUNS** is the sum of all of the previous three statistics.

Pitchers

Let's give our pitchers a turn, using 2020 AL Cy Young winner Shane Bieber as our example. Take a look at his stat block: the first line and the **YEAR**, **TEAM**, **LVL** and **AGE** columns are the same as in the position player example earlier.

Here too, we have a series of columns that display raw, unadjusted statistics compiled by the pitcher over the course of a season: **W** (wins), **L** (losses), **SV** (saves), **G** (games pitched), **GS** (games started), **IP** (innings pitched), **H** (hits allowed) and **HR** (home runs allowed). Next we have two statistics that are rates: **BB/9** (walks per nine innings) and **K/9** (strikeouts per nine innings), before returning to the unadjusted K (strikeouts).

Next up is **GB%** (ground ball percentage), which is the percentage of all batted balls that were hit on the ground, including both outs and hits. Remember, this is based on observational data and subject to human error, so please approach this with a healthy dose of skepticism.

BABIP (batting average on balls in play) is calculated using the same methodology as it is for position players, but it often tells us more about a pitcher than it does a hitter. With pitchers, a high BABIP is often due to poor defense or bad luck, and can often be an indicator of potential rebound, and a low BABIP may be cause to expect performance regression. (A typical league-average BABIP is close to .290-.300.)

The metrics **WHIP** (walks plus hits per inning pitched) and **ERA** (earned run average) are old standbys: WHIP measures walks and hits allowed on a per-inning basis, while ERA measures earned runs on a nine-inning basis. Neither of these stats are translated or adjusted.

DRA- (Deserved Run Average) was described at length earlier, and measures how the pitcher "deserved" to perform compared to other pitchers. Please note that since we lack all the data points that would make for a "real" DRA for minor-league events, the DRA- displayed for minor league partial-seasons is based off of different data. (That data is a modified version of our cFIP metric, which you can find more information about on our website.)

Shane Bieber   RHP

Born: 05/31/95   Age: 26   Bats: R   Throws: R
Height: 6'3"   Weight: 200   Origin: Round 4, 2016 Draft (#122 overall)

YEAR	TEAM	LVL	AGE	W	L	SV	G	GS	IP	H	HR	BB/9	K/9	K	GB%	BABIP
2018	AKR	AA	23	3	0	0	5	5	31	26	1	0.3	8.7	30	47.3%	.278
2018	COL	AAA	23	3	1	0	8	8	48[2]	30	3	1.1	8.7	47	52.0%	.227
2018	CLE	MLB	23	11	5	0	20	19	114[2]	130	13	1.8	9.3	118	46.2%	.356
2019	CLE	MLB	24	15	8	0	34	33	214[1]	186	31	1.7	10.9	259	44.4%	.298
2020	CLE	MLB	25	8	1	0	12	12	77[1]	46	7	2.4	14.2	122	48.4%	.267
2021 FS	CLE	MLB	26	10	6	0	26	26	150	121	18	2.1	11.7	195	45.5%	.297
2021 DC	CLE	MLB	26	14	7	0	30	30	196.7	159	24	2.1	11.7	257	45.5%	.297

Comparables: Luis Severino, Danny Salazar, Joe Musgrove

YEAR	TEAM	LVL	AGE	WHIP	ERA	DRA-	WARP	MPH	FB%	WHF	CSP
2018	AKR	AA	23	0.87	1.16	61	0.9				
2018	COL	AAA	23	0.74	1.66	69	1.2				
2018	CLE	MLB	23	1.33	4.55	74	2.6	94.7	57.4%	26.2%	
2019	CLE	MLB	24	1.05	3.28	75	4.9	94.4	45.8%	30.8%	
2020	CLE	MLB	25	0.87	1.63	53	2.6	95.3	53.6%	40.7%	
2021 FS	CLE	MLB	26	1.04	2.44	64	4.4	94.7	50.0%	33.2%	44.2%
2021 DC	CLE	MLB	26	1.04	2.44	64	5.8	94.7	50.0%	33.2%	44.2%

Just like with hitters, **WARP** (Wins Above Replacement Player) is a total value metric that puts pitchers of all stripes on the same scale as position players. We use DRA as the primary input for our calculation of WARP. You might notice that relief pitchers (due to their limited innings) may have a lower WARP than you were expecting or than you might see in other WARP-like metrics. WARP does not take leverage into account, just the actions a pitcher performs and the expected value of those actions ... which ends up judging high-leverage relief pitchers differently than you might imagine given their prestige and market value.

MPH gives you the pitcher's 95th percentile velocity for the noted season, in order to give you an idea of what the *peak* fastball velocity a pitcher possesses. Since this comes from our pitch-tracking data, it is not publicly available for minor-league pitchers.

Finally, we display the three new pitching metrics we described earlier. **FB%** (fastball percentage) gives you the percentage of fastballs thrown out of all pitches. **WHF** (whiff rate) tells you the percentage of swinging strikes induced out of all pitches. **CSP** (called strike probability) expresses the likelihood of all pitches thrown to result in a called strike, after controlling for factors like handedness, umpire, pitch type, count and location.

PECOTA

All players have PECOTA projections for 2021, as well as a set of other numbers that describe the performance of comparable players according to PECOTA. All projections for 2021 are for the player at the date we went to press in early January and are projected into the league and park context as indicated by the team abbreviation. (Note that players at very low levels of the minors are too unpredictable to assess using these numbers.) All PECOTA projected statistics represent a player's projected major-league performance.

How we're doing that is a little different this season. There are really two different values that go into the final stat line that you see for PECOTA: How a player performs, and how much playing time he'll be given to perform it. In the past we've estimated playing time based on each team's roster and depth charts, and we'll continue to do that. These projections are denoted as **2021 DC**.

But in many cases, a player won't be projected for major-league playing time; most of the time this is because they aren't projected to be major-league players at all, but still developing as prospects. Or perhaps a player will provide Triple-A depth, only to have an opportunity open up because of injury. For these purposes, we're also supplying a second projection, labeled **2021 FS**, or full season. This is what we would project the player to provide in 600 plate appearances or 150 innings pitched.

Below the projections are the player's three highest-scoring comparable players as determined by PECOTA. All comparables represent a snapshot of how the listed player was performing at the same age as the current player, so if a

23-year-old pitcher is compared to Bartolo Colón, he's actually being compared to a 23-year-old Colón, not the version that pitched for the Rangers in 2018, nor to Colón's career as a whole.

A few points about pitcher projections. First, we aren't yet projecting peak velocity, so that column will be blank in the PECOTA lines. Second, projecting DRA is trickier than evaluating past performance, because it is unclear how deserving each pitcher will be of his anticipated outcomes. However, we know that another DRA-related statistic–contextual FIP or cFIP-estimates future run scoring very well. So for PECOTA, the projected DRA- figures you see are based on the past cFIPs generated by the pitcher and comparable players over time, along with the other factors described above.

If you're familiar with PECOTA, then you'll have noticed that the projection system often appears bullish on players coming off a bad year and bearish on players coming off a good year. (This is because the system weights several previous seasons, not just the most recent one.) In addition, we publish the 50th percentile projections for each player–which is smack in the middle of the range of projected production—which tends to mean PECOTA stat lines don't often have extreme results like 40 home runs or 250 strikeouts in a given season. In essence, PECOTA doesn't project very many extreme seasons.

Managers

After all those wonderful team chapters, we've got statistics for each big-league manager, all of whom are organized by alphabetical order. Here you'll find a block including an extraordinary amount of information collected from each manager's entire career. For more information on the acronyms and what they mean, please visit the Glossary at www.baseballprospectus.com.

There is one important metric that we'd like to call attention to, and you'll find it next to each manager's name: **wRM+** (weighted reliever management plus). Developed by Rob Arthur and Rian Watt, wRM+ investigates how good a manager is at using their best relievers during the moments of highest leverage, using both our proprietary DRA metric as well as Leverage Index. wRM+ is scaled to a league average of 100, and a wRM+ of 105 indicates that relievers were used approximately five percent "better" than average. On the other hand, a wRM+ of 95 would tell us the team used its relievers five percent "worse" than the average team.

While wRM+ does not have an extremely strong correlation with a manager, it is statistically significant; this means that a manager is not *entirely* responsible for a team's wRM+, but does have some effect on that number.

Part 1: Team Analysis

Performance Graphs

Payroll History (in millions)

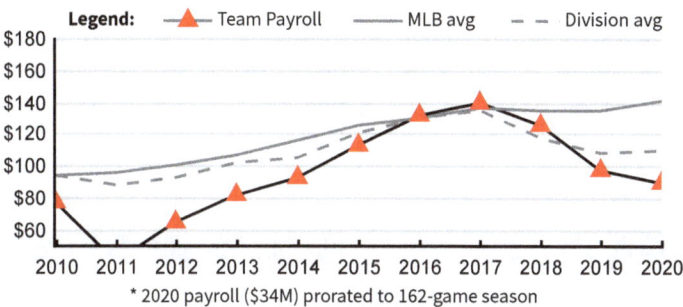

* 2020 payroll ($34M) prorated to 162-game season

Future Commitments (in millions)

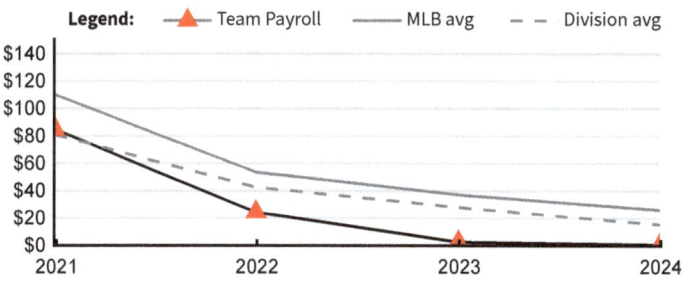

Farm System Ranking

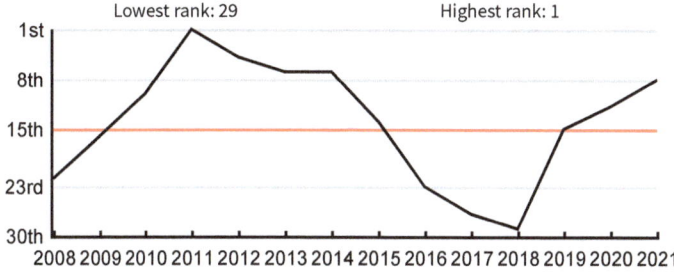

2020 Team Performance

ACTUAL STANDINGS

Team	W	L	Pct
MIN	36	24	0.600
CHW	35	25	0.583
CLE	35	25	0.583
KC	**26**	**34**	**0.433**
DET	23	35	0.397

dWIN% STANDINGS

Team	W	L	Pct
CLE	30	30	0.506
MIN	29	31	0.498
CHW	27	33	0.456
KC	**24**	**36**	**0.403**
DET	19	41	0.333

TOP HITTERS

Player	WARP
Whit Merrifield	1.2
Salvador Perez	1.1
Nicky Lopez	0.6

TOP PITCHERS

Player	WARP
Brady Singer	1.0
Brad Keller	0.7
Scott Barlow	0.7

VITAL STATISTICS

Statistic Name	Value	Rank
Pythagenpat	.457	22nd
dWin%	.403	24th
Runs Scored per Game	4.13	26th
Runs Allowed per Game	4.53	13th
Deserved Runs Created Plus	91	27th
Deserved Run Average Minus	101	18th
Fielding Independent Pitching	4.57	18th
Defensive Efficiency Rating	.690	22nd
Batter Age	28.4	15th
Pitcher Age	27.7	6th
Payroll	$34.0M	27th
Marginal $ per Marginal Win	$2.0M	9th

2021 Team Projections

PROJECTED STANDINGS

Team	W	L	Pct	+/-
MIN	90.8	71.2	0.560	-6
With Nelson Cruz returning and Andrelton Simmons, J.A. Happ, and Alex Colomé on board the Twins seem like a balanced behemoth again.				
CLE	85.0	77.0	0.525	-9
That they've lost so many great players is an indictment of ownership. That they remain respectable is a testament to the agility of the front office.				
CHW	82.8	79.2	0.511	-11
Lance Lynn and Liam Hendriks give Tony La Russa the paint-by-numbers pitching staff he prefers, and all of the crucial cogs in last year's young lineup return.				
KC	**71.5**	**90.5**	**0.441**	**1**
Creeping back toward respectability, the Royals added reliable veterans coming off down years and will hope their youth movement gains momentum quickly.				
DET	65.7	96.3	0.406	3
The trend arrow is finally pointing up, but Robbie Grossman and Wilson Ramos qualifying as significant improvements shows they still have a long way to go.				

TOP PROJECTED HITTERS

Player	WARP
Jorge Soler	2.6
Whit Merrifield	2.3
Carlos Santana	2.2

TOP PROJECTED PITCHERS

Player	WARP
Mike Minor	1.9
Brady Singer	1.5
Brad Keller	1.3

FARM SYSTEM REPORT

Top Prospect	Number of Top 101 Prospects
Bobby Witt Jr., #9	5

KEY DEDUCTIONS

Player	WARP
Franchy Cordero	1.2

KEY ADDITIONS

Player	WARP
Carlos Santana	2.2
Mike Minor	1.9
Andrew Benintendi	1.5
Michael A. Taylor	0.4

Team Personnel

Senior Vice President - Baseball Operations/General Manager
Dayton Moore

Assistant General Manager of Player Personnel
J.J. Picollo

Assistant General Manager of Major League and International Operations
Rene Francisco

Assistant General Manager
Scott Sharp

Manager
Mike Matheny

BP Alumni
Daniel Mack

Kauffman Stadium Stats

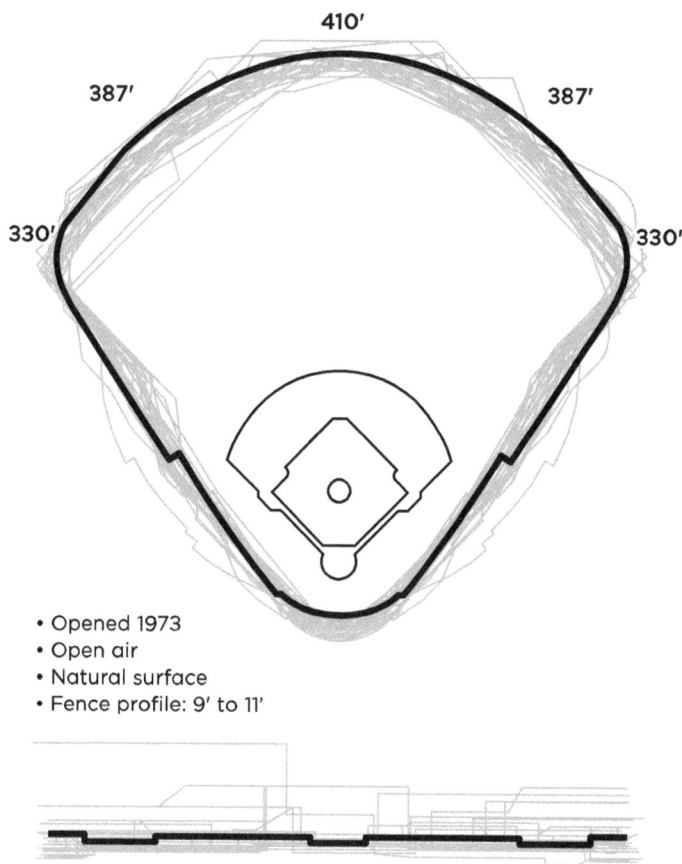

- Opened 1973
- Open air
- Natural surface
- Fence profile: 9' to 11'

Three-Year Park Factors

Runs	Runs/RH	Runs/LH	HR/RH	HR/LH
100	100	101	90	92

Royals Team Analysis

Pssst!

You there, in the Mahomes jersey! Come join me over here, by the fountain!

You know, I've been called a lot of things in my time: A scoundrel. A wastrel. A Kansas City flimflam man. The "Harold Hill" of committing crimes without a marching band. But when the summertime comes, I'm just a baseball fan like the rest of you.

Speaking of which, what would you do if I told you there's a ball team—right here in town, in fact—that's got the guts to recreate itself, but the fortitude not to surrender? That's got a skipper who earned his playing time with a mouthful of blood? That has a general manager ready to shield his boys from the sweet embrace of adult films?

Would you say, "Golly, that's a club I'd give my eyeballs for an afternoon!"

Well, get ready to soothe those sockets, friend—the 2021 Royals are playing at home tonight! And I've got a pair of tickets, just for you.

For a fair price, of course.

You're "too busy?" For *baseball*? The sport our forefathers played with broomsticks and wads of rubber bands in the street, using open manholes for bases? The sport that brought America together one magical summer with only a couple dozen dingers and a handful of pills? The game that Rob Manfred fell so head-over-Florsheims in love with, he can't even talk about it without his mouth crinkling into that thing he calls a smile? The pastime that was so important to this country that after two major in-season viral outbreaks, the league decided the only cure was to *keep playing baseball??*

Nobody's "too busy" for baseball around here. You could be lazing in a sun-drenched Kauffman Stadium seat this very night, taking in this game of kings and knaves. The Royals play a style of ball that's swift, pure and American; which may explain why they lose so often. Heh, heh.

Lighten up, pal. You're blind as an umpire if you don't see our great nation taking some L's. The trick is to not take too many in a row.

Kansas City Royals 2021

In fact, I know what you're thinking: "Didn't these Royals just lose over a hundred games? That sounds like a lot!" Well, check the papers, friend. They've lost over *two* hundred in the past three seasons. But *this* Royals team is different. This team is going to *win*. Why? Because they *deserve* to. And when's the last time America didn't get what it deserved?

It's coming back to you now, isn't it? "Wasn't this team in the World Series just five short years ago?" They sure were, pal. Won the whole thing, too. That was a fast bunch. Didn't homer a ton. Knew how to flip the leather. Pinch ran like they had a track team on the bench. But time is mean for no reason, and those days are long behind us now.

Those boys are gone, is my point. Salvador Perez is still here, at least; sure, his tendons have been moved around a bit, but the old man can still thrill a cardboard cutout or two. But even Alex Gordon has packed it up and headed back to the flatlands to sip tea and watch the sunset over the plains. Sure, he deserves it, but it's difficult to watch him go.

You know what happens when teams break apart in baseball, don't you? Well, what happens in *any* business when the numbers are down? Any sensible businessman would be giving the place a gasoline shower and having a smoke. Then, it's time to collect on the insurance and start a new life. In baseball, we call that "rebuilding."

The Royals may seem like they're doing that, but according to them at the beginning of the 2020 season—they're not! I heard Dayton Moore and Mike Matheny will throw a chair if they hear the word "rebuild" so much as whispered by the breeze. In fact, I'm not sure if we should even be talking about this. Anybody asks, we're just a couple of fellas standing here, having a good old fashioned how's-your-mother.

Anyway, what was I saying? Oh, right—Moore went off like a dog at the moon when somebody brought up his Royals rebuilding; all *"We are done with that,"* and *"We have an obligation to win as many games as possible,"* and even, *"There is an expectation for these players to perform and to win. That's what we're here for."* I think that last one's straight from the good book itself. The Bible Belt isn't just a place, y'know; it's what's holding up Dayton Moore's pants.

The point is, these Royals weren't some bunch of torpid layabouts in 2020, preening in the sun like Missouri street lizards. These were fully charged batsmen with steam coming out of their ears for nine innings. Did they win a lot of games? They did not. Did they score a lot of runs? They did not. But as they pushed onward, future champions emerged and the vision of glory in the days ahead began to form like an honest-to-God Rockefeller painting for all those still watching.

Just take this Adalberto Mondesi, why don't you. Kid's got a head full of snakes. He led the league in swiping bases that didn't belong to him, and you better believe the other teams hated it. Brady Singer didn't allow a run for 14 straight innings. Kris Bubic was among the rookie strikeout leaders. Word is, somewhere in Nebraska they've got a warehouse packed with fresh-armed studs, flourishing like the miles and miles of government corn surrounding them. I hadn't ever seen more intimidating youths in one place since that gang of street urchins surrounded me in a boxcar.

Change is inevitable, pal. You know it, same as I did the day I woke up with a bunch of preteens hoisting me in the air, about to throw me from a moving train. During a time like this for a team, the clubhouse becomes a junction of swiftly forgotten substitutes, auditioners, prospects, hangers-on, blackguards and ragamuffins. Old favorites depart, new faces arrive, players are packaged up and shipped out of town. The manager is one of the only constants, overseeing every step forward and backward: a stoic presence, nodding sagely from the doorway of his office as the team takes shape.

Friend, meet Mike Matheny. In 2012 he was on the other side of the Show-Me with the Cardinals, where he was a first-time manager, a former lousy hitter and a defensive catcher who was once hit in the face with a fastball. This was a battle-hardened, punch-taking, star-spangled roughneck; the kind of fellow who gets handed the key to his hometown. I had a front row seat to that show for a while, hanging around outside the players entrance—Joe Kelly used to pay me to find "cool rocks" for him throw at trains—and let me tell you: Matheny was a man who made up for his lack of leadership skills with a strong desire to have better leadership skills.

After being hired by the Royals, Matheny was celebrated for looking at the flaws in his managerial style and trying to improve between his first job and his second one, going so far as to enroll in a ten-week online baseball analytics course. Did you know they can fit college inside a computer now? Incredible stuff.

He's got something few other managers do: A published manifesto. Thomas Paine! Edmund Burke! Karl Marx! Mike Matheny! They all had ideas too powerful to live exclusively in their brains; ideas to recalibrate society, to rebel against tyrants, and in Matheny's case, to suggest not screaming at children while coaching youth sports.

Matheny was definitely in it to win it in 2020, very nearly almost half the time, making more moves per game than any other manager in baseball. That meant more steal attempts, more bunts, more pinch hitters, more relief pitchers, more action. Matheny was a manager who was trying to *manage*. Was it successful? Friend, what's more exciting, the runner taking off for second or getting tagged out at the end? Life is all about anticipation. What's important is that the Royals are *not* rebuilding. They are re-expecting to win. Just like they always have. And they've got the perfect manager to do that.

Kansas City Royals 2021

Did you know that the first game in Kansas City Royals history was a thrilling, 4-3 walk-off win? Once it was finally over, it was a great relief to those watching. They'd feared, as the absurd game entered its twelfth inning and fourth hour, that this whole baseball thing meant a lifetime sentence.

And how about that last game in Kansas City Royals history? A victorious, 3-1 season finale, twice-delayed; the first time for three months due to the pandemic, and the second time for 95 minutes due to rain. Once it was finally over, it was a great relief to those watching, as earlier in the year, fans had wondered when they'd ever see a baseball season completed again.

So you see? Baseball—watching it, playing it, deciding whether or not it should continue during a pandemic—is all about finding that narrow margin between too much and too little into which you can wedge yourself. Me? I wedge myself into a crawl space every night, because it's the only way I feel safe in the dark. Plus, if any gangs of children are looking for me, they can't reach that high with their scrawny, emaciated arms.

Forgive me for getting philosophical, but I guess that's kind of like life now: Cramming our slovenly existences into smaller and smaller spaces. It's made it easier to forget what we used to recognize. Baseball dropped 102 games off its schedule in 2020 in the name of public health and safety and became a manic 60-game carnival with basically no rules. That's not the always-thrilling, well-managed, competently-overseen baseball I know! So for the Royals, for the league, for everybody; 2020 was all about the potential to get things right. Eventually. And now 2021 is here, to continue that potential.

So you see: Baseball's not just about knowing who you are! It's knowing who you *could* be!

Tell me, chum; when you get up in the morning, your hair askew, lips parched, eyes shot with blood from another sleepless night in plague times, do you see yourself in that mirror and think, "Yep, that's me all right!"

No! You give yourself a few slaps, scream into a pillow, put on your best suit and tie and strap in for another industrious day in the living room.

That's our Royals, friend—not some deluded bunch of powder blue porn-haters! Well, not entirely. They're fully aware of how they woke up this morning; only instead of tossing fitfully between nightmares last night, they lost 241 baseball games. And they're still getting up for work, just like you.

So when they say they're not rebuilding, when they say they're here to win, you believe them! I sure do! In this league, you don't keep signing guys named "Mike" because you're trying to lose.

Now, whether or not they succeed is entirely different. But believing is half the battle! The other half is evaluating and developing talent up the middle; stockpiling several generations' worth of pitchers; fortifying franchise infrastructure; properly timing the promotions of top prospects; acquiring the right free agents to fill in the gaps; and getting the nod from ownership to spend like your hair's on fire, if need be.

Yes, you're right. That's a lot of things to jam into one half. But "believing" deserves to be its own half of the process, because it's hard! Just ask anyone who has ever given up on anything—a job, a project, a person. They're everywhere!

So, go ahead. Take the tickets for tonight's game. We can work out a fair price for them, I'm sure. What's the going rate for a train ticket out of town? I'd settle for that. I'm looking forward to stepping onboard, rather than running alongside with the sheriff on my tail.

Excellent. Friend, you won't regret this. Baseball is all about believing in the potential of the seemingly impossible. It's a lot like life in that way, don't you think? And when life gets bad, we all need those nine innings to believe in something on occasion, don't we? Things like, *what if that run comes into score even those there's two outs, or maybe we'll someday live in a world where attending a baseball game doesn't require you to sign a document clearing MLB of liability if you get sick and die.*

Before we part, friend, let me level with you. I've learned a few lessons walking these streets in my sharp tie and brimmed cap. One is: Never wager with a man who is ready to die.

But the biggest lesson I've learned is that when the world starts taking things from you, what you manage to hang onto matters so much more. While billionaires the world over scrambled to protect themselves after COVID, Royals bigwigs did the unthinkable and instituted pay cuts at the executive level only, preventing them from having to make layoffs or furloughs to team employees. That move told anybody watching that while the world had changed, the Royals had maintained what was important to them: Keeping their people employed.

Isn't that beautiful? Sorry. I need a moment.

Come, let's stare into the churning flow of this fountain together and think about how nice that is. Maybe we can toss in a penny or a quarter or a fifty dollar bill and make a wish. I'm fresh out of cash, though, so why don't you just go ahead and toss your largest bill in there. I'll stay behind and make sure no one fishes it out.

Say, was that a train whistle? I better catch it. Take care, friend, and remember: You can't win 'em all; but you can try to. And that's a lot like winning itself. Except for the score. And the outcome. And the standings.

Farewell!

—*Justin Klugh is an author of Baseball Prospectus.*

Part 2: Player Analysis

Kansas City Royals 2021

PLAYER COMMENTS WITH GRAPHS

Hanser Alberto 2B
Born: 10/17/92 Age: 28 Bats: R Throws: R
Height: 5'11" Weight: 215 Origin: International Free Agent, 2009

YEAR	TEAM	LVL	AGE	PA	R	2B	3B	HR	RBI	BB	K	SB	CS	AVG/OBP/SLG
2018	RR	AAA	25	384	45	17	3	7	58	9	28	0	3	.330/.346/.452
2018	TEX	MLB	25	30	0	2	0	0	0	2	4	0	1	.185/.241/.259
2019	BAL	MLB	26	550	62	21	2	12	51	16	50	4	4	.305/.329/.422
2020	BAL	MLB	27	231	35	15	0	3	22	5	30	3	0	.283/.306/.393
2021 FS	KC	MLB	28	600	54	26	2	11	61	19	88	3	2	.265/.294/.382
2021 DC	KC	MLB	28	173	15	7	0	3	17	5	25	0	1	.265/.294/.382

Comparables: Jose Lopez, Mel Roach, Jerry Adair

There were more egregious examples of deplorable thriftiness across the league on a depressing non-tender deadline day, but the Birds cutting bait with their leadoff hitter to save a few million still deserves a heavy, exasperated, "MLB's economic system is seriously screwed up" sigh. Alberto is a beautifully flawed player; in 2020 he had the league's fourth-worst average exit velocity and one of its best strikeout rates, and he absolutely crushed lefties. That bizarre offensive profile, plus his average defense at second and third makes him the epitome of a league-average player—something of which the 2021 Orioles could use a few. He was a fan favorite: a distinctive, watchable baseball man and a reason to turn on MASN. Alberto probably wasn't going to be a member of the next good Orioles team, but he still should have been a member of the next bad Orioles team. Chances are he makes it through next season with two strikeouts, no batted balls over 85 mph and a .400 average against lefties. Chapeau, Hanser.

YEAR	TEAM	LVL	AGE	PA	DRC+	BABIP	BRR	FRAA	WARP
2018	RR	AAA	25	384	111	.337	-0.8	SS(44): 7.1, 1B(43): -3.5, 2B(9): 1.7	1.5
2018	TEX	MLB	25	30	88	.217	-0.4	SS(5): 0.1, 2B(4): -0.1, 3B(3): -0.0	0.0
2019	BAL	MLB	26	550	97	.318	1.6	2B(90): -5.0, 3B(66): 5.3, LF(3): -0.1	2.0
2020	BAL	MLB	27	231	85	.314	0.2	2B(52): -3.2, 3B(5): 0.6	0.2
2021 FS	KC	MLB	28	600	86	.295	-0.5	2B -1, 3B 2	0.4
2021 DC	KC	MLB	28	173	86	.295	-0.2	2B 0, 3B 1	0.1

Hanser Alberto, continued

Batted Ball Distribution

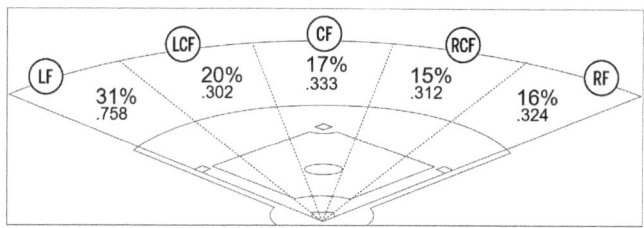

Strike Zone vs LHP   Strike Zone vs RHP

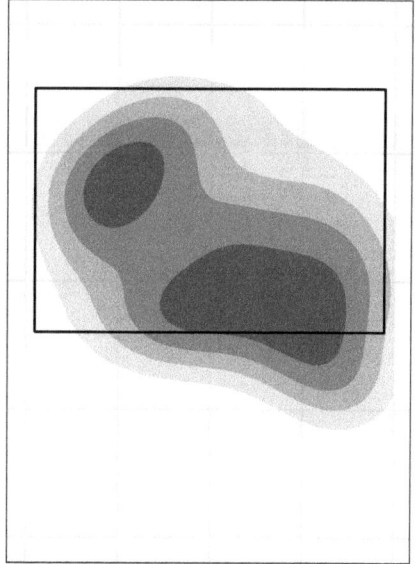

Kansas City Royals 2021

Hunter Dozier   3B

Born: 08/22/91   Age: 29   Bats: R   Throws: R
Height: 6'4"   Weight: 220   Origin: Round 1, 2013 Draft (#8 overall)

YEAR	TEAM	LVL	AGE	PA	R	2B	3B	HR	RBI	BB	K	SB	CS	AVG/OBP/SLG
2018	OMA	AAA	26	143	18	7	0	1	11	24	43	2	1	.254/.385/.339
2018	KC	MLB	26	388	36	19	4	11	34	24	109	2	3	.229/.278/.395
2019	KC	MLB	27	586	75	29	10	26	84	55	148	2	2	.279/.348/.522
2020	KC	MLB	28	186	29	4	2	6	12	27	48	4	0	.228/.344/.392
2021 FS	KC	MLB	29	600	72	25	5	19	69	62	175	2	2	.235/.318/.414
2021 DC	KC	MLB	29	578	69	24	4	18	66	59	169	2	2	.235/.318/.414

Comparables: Butch Hobson, Bill Hall, Nick Castellanos

A COVID-19 casualty at the end of summer camp, Dozier struggled offensively once he returned to the lineup. His exit velocity was down and his hard-hit rate tumbled to 10 points below his career average. He was disciplined at the plate, chasing just a quarter of pitches out of the strikezone, but his whiff rate was elevated, especially against breaking pitches. Always a bit of a defensive nomad, wandering between the corners in the infield and the outfield, he found a home at first base. And as the Royals collected options for their outfield like a penny-pincher clipping coupons, the cold corner looks to be his most likely future home.

YEAR	TEAM	LVL	AGE	PA	DRC+	BABIP	BRR	FRAA	WARP
2018	OMA	AAA	26	143	115	.392	-0.2	3B(19): 0.6, RF(13): 1.2, 1B(4): -0.0	0.6
2018	KC	MLB	26	388	80	.296	-0.3	1B(51): -7.5, 3B(37): -5.9, RF(2): -0.0	-1.5
2019	KC	MLB	27	586	118	.339	-1.8	3B(100): -0.3, RF(20): 0.4, 1B(7): -0.8	3.0
2020	KC	MLB	28	186	103	.288	0.9	1B(28): -0.8, RF(18): -0.5, LF(2): 0.1	0.3
2021 FS	KC	MLB	29	600	104	.311	0.0	3B -1, LF 0	1.3
2021 DC	KC	MLB	29	578	104	.311	0.0	3B -1, LF 0	1.3

Hunter Dozier, continued

Batted Ball Distribution

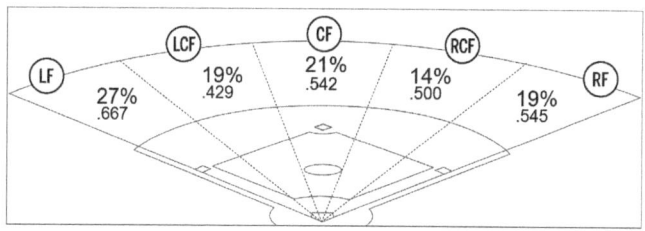

Strike Zone vs LHP   Strike Zone vs RHP

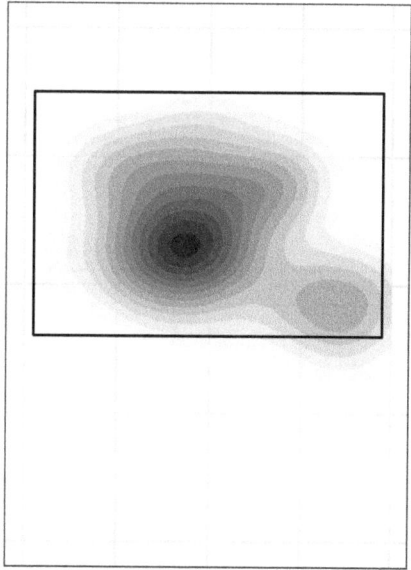

Royals Player Analysis - 19

Kansas City Royals 2021

Maikel Franco 3B

Born: 08/26/92 Age: 28 Bats: R Throws: R
Height: 6'1" Weight: 225 Origin: International Free Agent, 2010

YEAR	TEAM	LVL	AGE	PA	R	2B	3B	HR	RBI	BB	K	SB	CS	AVG/OBP/SLG
2018	PHI	MLB	25	465	48	17	1	22	68	29	62	1	0	.270/.314/.467
2019	LHV	AAA	26	46	5	2	1	2	6	5	7	0	0	.175/.283/.425
2019	PHI	MLB	26	428	48	17	0	17	56	36	61	0	0	.234/.297/.409
2020	KC	MLB	27	243	23	16	0	8	38	16	38	1	0	.278/.321/.457
2021 FS	KC	MLB	28	600	64	28	1	20	72	44	103	0	1	.248/.305/.417

Comparables: Joe Crede, Aramis Ramirez, Mike Moustakas

Freed from the yoke of expectations that accompanied him in Philadelphia, Franco settled into the Royals lineup—and clubhouse—and enjoyed his best overall offensive season since 2015. It wasn't happenstance. After signing with Kansas City, he made his way to Miami for some offseason hitting work with Royals hitting coaches Pedro Grifol and Mike Tosar. The result: His average exit velocity on batted balls was down, but he made more regular—and solid—contact, increasing his line drive rate by a third. A resulting bump in his BABIP followed and he was a mainstay for the Royals in the heart of their order. He also made hay against lefties, something he hasn't done consistently over his career.

YEAR	TEAM	LVL	AGE	PA	DRC+	BABIP	BRR	FRAA	WARP
2018	PHI	MLB	25	465	109	.270	1.5	3B(117): -2.7	2.1
2019	LHV	AAA	26	46	83	.161	-0.3	3B(11): 0.9	0.1
2019	PHI	MLB	26	428	88	.236	-1.0	3B(110): 2.5, 1B(2): -0.0	1.1
2020	KC	MLB	27	243	104	.298	-0.2	3B(51): -1.8, 1B(2): -0.0	0.3
2021 FS	KC	MLB	28	600	100	.270	-0.8	3B 0, 1B 0	1.0

Maikel Franco, continued

Batted Ball Distribution

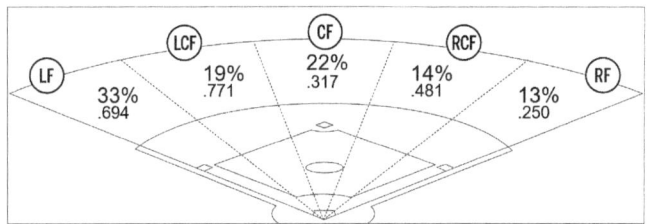

Strike Zone vs LHP   **Strike Zone vs RHP**

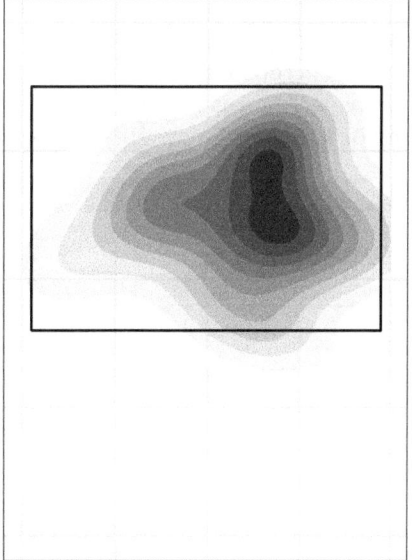

Alex Gordon LF

Born: 02/10/84 Age: 37 Bats: L Throws: R
Height: 6'1" Weight: 220 Origin: Round 1, 2005 Draft (#2 overall)

YEAR	TEAM	LVL	AGE	PA	R	2B	3B	HR	RBI	BB	K	SB	CS	AVG/OBP/SLG
2018	KC	MLB	34	568	56	24	0	13	54	50	124	12	2	.245/.324/.370
2019	KC	MLB	35	633	77	31	1	13	76	51	100	5	3	.266/.345/.396
2020	KC	MLB	36	184	15	4	0	4	11	18	37	0	0	.209/.299/.307
2021 FS	KC	MLB	37	600	59	21	1	13	58	57	147	8	4	.215/.310/.336
2021 DC	KC	MLB	37	350	34	12	0	7	33	33	85	4	3	.215/.310/.336

Comparables: Cliff Floyd, Greg Vaughn, Gus Zernial

In many ways, Gordon's career mirrored the fortunes of the Royals. Drafted as a third baseman, he scuffled, struggled and underachieved through his first several seasons in Kansas City. A brief exile to Triple-A, a position shift and a relationship with Rusty Kuntz transformed him into one of the top outfielders in the league during his prime. As the Royals shot up the American League ranks and reached the pinnacle, he was the steady veteran presence; the leader by example. The ninth-inning dinger to tie Game One of the 2015 World Series against closer Jeurys Familia will forever be an iconic moment of that championship season. The last five years haven't been as kind, as injury and age once again conspired against a top athlete; retirement beckoned. Someday, his number will be enshrined alongside other Royal icons George Brett, Frank White and Dick Howser. Enjoy retirement—and the pizza—Gordo.

YEAR	TEAM	LVL	AGE	PA	DRC+	BABIP	BRR	FRAA	WARP
2018	KC	MLB	34	568	89	.299	-1.9	LF(125): 3.3, CF(11): -0.9, RF(1): 0.1	0.8
2019	KC	MLB	35	633	96	.301	0.6	LF(146): -2.7, P(2): -0.0	1.2
2020	KC	MLB	36	184	83	.246	0.1	LF(49): 1.5	0.5
2021 FS	KC	MLB	37	600	81	.274	0.0	LF 3, CF 0	0.3
2021 DC	KC	MLB	37	350	81	.274	0.0	LF 1, CF 0	0.2

Alex Gordon, continued

Batted Ball Distribution

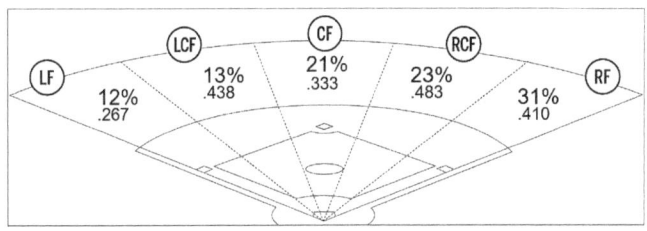

Strike Zone vs LHP   Strike Zone vs RHP

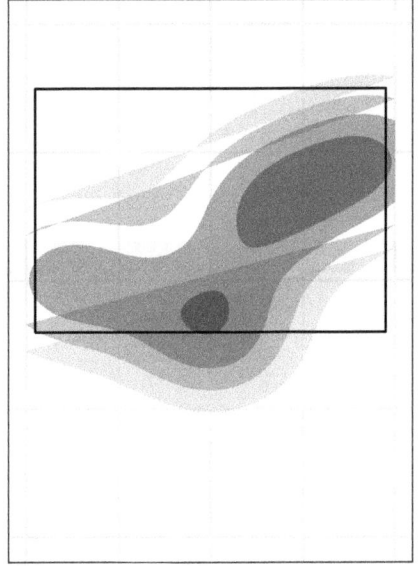 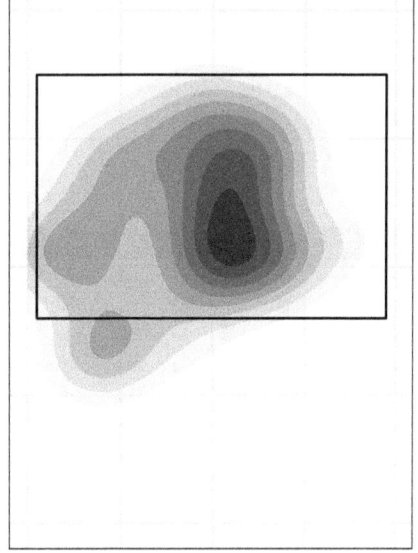

Nicky Lopez 2B

Born: 03/13/95 Age: 26 Bats: L Throws: R
Height: 5'11" Weight: 175 Origin: Round 5, 2016 Draft (#163 overall)

YEAR	TEAM	LVL	AGE	PA	R	2B	3B	HR	RBI	BB	K	SB	CS	AVG/OBP/SLG
2018	NWA	AA	23	325	42	8	5	2	27	33	23	9	4	.331/.397/.416
2018	OMA	AAA	23	256	33	6	2	7	26	27	29	6	2	.278/.364/.417
2019	OMA	AAA	24	138	27	6	1	3	13	20	5	9	3	.353/.457/.500
2019	KC	MLB	24	402	44	22	2	2	30	18	51	1	1	.240/.276/.325
2020	KC	MLB	25	192	15	8	0	1	13	18	41	0	5	.201/.286/.266
2021 FS	KC	MLB	26	600	62	27	4	8	54	49	110	8	3	.245/.315/.357
2021 DC	KC	MLB	26	442	46	20	3	6	40	36	81	5	3	.245/.315/.357

Comparables: Brad Wellman, Mark Grudzielanek, Tilson Brito

Let's go for the positive and start with the defense. Lopez excelled at the keystone, exhibiting excellent range and a killer double play pivot. The glovework was worth eight Defensive Runs Saved, tops in the AL at his position, and garnered a nomination for a Gold Glove. That's the good. Now for the … less positive. Coming up through the minors, Lopez was a grinder at the plate, battling every plate appearance, drawing walks at an above-average clip while keeping strikeouts at bay. But that approach hasn't materialized in the majors. With a depressed on-base percentage, another issue is he just doesn't make hard contact. His average exit velocity ranked 189 out of 194 batters who put more than 100 balls in play in 2020 and he ranked in the 96th percentile in outs above average. In other words, he's an out machine on both offense and defense.

YEAR	TEAM	LVL	AGE	PA	DRC+	BABIP	BRR	FRAA	WARP
2018	NWA	AA	23	325	123	.351	2.8	SS(58): -4.8, 2B(14): 0.4	1.2
2018	OMA	AAA	23	256	120	.294	0.0	SS(36): -1.0, 2B(18): 1.7	1.3
2019	OMA	AAA	24	138	139	.352	-1.3	SS(17): 3.5, 2B(14): 1.0	1.5
2019	KC	MLB	24	402	61	.273	2.5	2B(76): 1.3, SS(33): 1.2	0.0
2020	KC	MLB	25	192	73	.260	-0.6	2B(53): 6.3, SS(4): 0.1, 3B(2): -0.0	0.6
2021 FS	KC	MLB	26	600	84	.296	0.4	2B 3, 3B 0	0.9
2021 DC	KC	MLB	26	442	84	.296	0.3	2B 2	0.7

Nicky Lopez, continued

Batted Ball Distribution

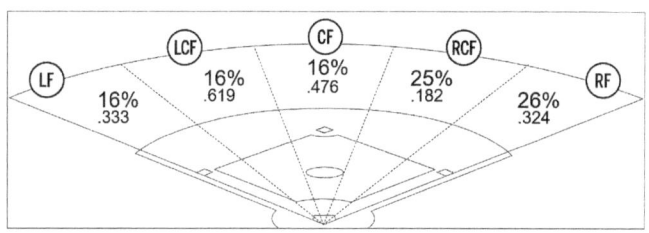

Strike Zone vs LHP   **Strike Zone vs RHP**

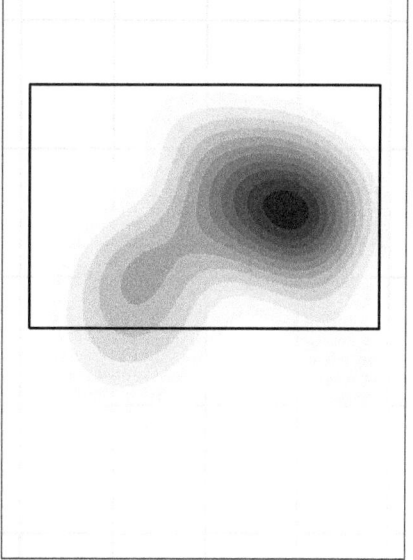

Ryan McBroom 1B

Born: 04/09/92 Age: 29 Bats: R Throws: L
Height: 6'3" Weight: 225 Origin: Round 15, 2014 Draft (#444 overall)

YEAR	TEAM	LVL	AGE	PA	R	2B	3B	HR	RBI	BB	K	SB	CS	AVG/OBP/SLG
2018	TRN	AA	26	111	13	5	1	4	14	7	27	0	3	.324/.378/.510
2018	SWB	AAA	26	393	49	18	1	11	46	25	106	1	4	.295/.339/.443
2019	SWB	AAA	27	482	87	29	0	26	66	58	100	2	2	.315/.402/.574
2019	KC	MLB	27	83	8	5	0	0	6	7	25	0	0	.293/.361/.360
2020	KC	MLB	28	85	8	3	0	6	10	4	30	0	0	.247/.282/.506
2021 FS	KC	MLB	29	600	67	23	1	23	74	43	192	0	1	.233/.297/.412
2021 DC	KC	MLB	29	32	3	1	0	1	3	2	10	0	0	.233/.297/.412

Comparables: Eric Munson, Bryan LaHair, Matt Clark

After opening the season as the right-handed hitting portion of a self-described "soft platoon" by the Royals, McBroom found himself spending the second half either on the bench or at the alternate site. He generally can hold his own against same-siders—hence the platoon being "soft"—but his offensive production was way down across the board.

YEAR	TEAM	LVL	AGE	PA	DRC+	BABIP	BRR	FRAA	WARP
2018	TRN	AA	26	111	133	.408	-0.4	1B(20): 0.9, RF(2): -0.1	0.4
2018	SWB	AAA	26	393	106	.383	-1.2	1B(45): -1.5, RF(34): 2.8, LF(9): -0.7	0.3
2019	SWB	AAA	27	482	141	.356	-3.8	1B(62): -1.2, RF(37): -0.3, LF(5): 0.5	2.6
2019	KC	MLB	27	83	72	.440	0.1	RF(12): -1.5, 1B(6): -0.5, LF(3): -0.1	-0.3
2020	KC	MLB	28	85	91	.311	-0.2	1B(10): -0.6, LF(3): -0.2, RF(1): 0.0	0.0
2021 FS	KC	MLB	29	600	97	.310	-0.9	1B -1, LF 0	0.6
2021 DC	KC	MLB	29	32	97	.310	0.0	1B 0	0.0

Ryan McBroom, continued

Batted Ball Distribution

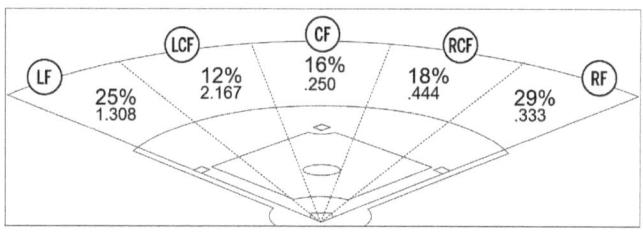

Strike Zone vs LHP   **Strike Zone vs RHP**

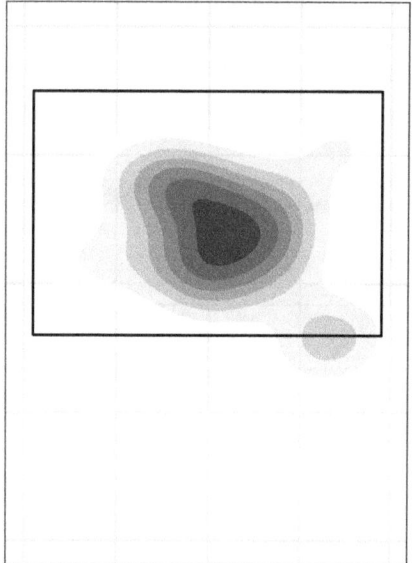

Whit Merrifield   RF

Born: 01/24/89   Age: 32   Bats: R   Throws: R
Height: 6'1"   Weight: 195   Origin: Round 9, 2010 Draft (#269 overall)

YEAR	TEAM	LVL	AGE	PA	R	2B	3B	HR	RBI	BB	K	SB	CS	AVG/OBP/SLG
2018	KC	MLB	29	707	88	43	3	12	60	61	114	45	10	.304/.367/.438
2019	KC	MLB	30	735	105	41	10	16	74	45	126	20	10	.302/.348/.463
2020	KC	MLB	31	265	38	12	0	9	30	12	33	12	3	.282/.325/.440
2021 FS	KC	MLB	32	600	78	29	4	14	55	37	100	24	8	.274/.325/.421
2021 DC	KC	MLB	32	661	86	32	4	16	60	41	110	26	9	.274/.325/.421

Comparables: Howie Kendrick, Brandon Phillips, Jeff Kent

Merrifield goes by the moniker "Two-Hit Whit" and with good reason. No hitter has had as many games with two hits or more over the last three seasons than his 133. Last year, he became a much more disciplined hitter, cutting down on his chase rate on pitches out of the zone while he upped his contact rate on pitches in the zone. Still, he must have done something to anger the BABIP gods as he endured a brutal 4-for-41 stretch in the middle of the year. Penance paid, he got back to that two-hit thing to close out the season on a high note. He's also something of a Swiss Army knife in the field, having logged time at five different positions in each of those last three years. And his sprint speed ranks in the 89th percentile. Is there anything he can't do? He is probably working on a cure for COVID-19 as you read this; that is if Dolly Parton hasn't already cracked it.

YEAR	TEAM	LVL	AGE	PA	DRC+	BABIP	BRR	FRAA	WARP
2018	KC	MLB	29	707	119	.352	3.5	2B(108): 2.3, CF(30): 1.4, RF(8): -0.1	4.4
2019	KC	MLB	30	735	109	.350	-1.9	2B(82): 6.2, RF(61): -6.4, CF(17): 1.5	3.0
2020	KC	MLB	31	265	113	.295	0.2	RF(34): 0.7, CF(23): 0.1, 2B(15): 1.5	1.2
2021 FS	KC	MLB	32	600	105	.310	1.9	RF -1, CF 1	2.3
2021 DC	KC	MLB	32	661	105	.310	2.1	RF -1, CF 1	2.3

Whit Merrifield, continued

Batted Ball Distribution

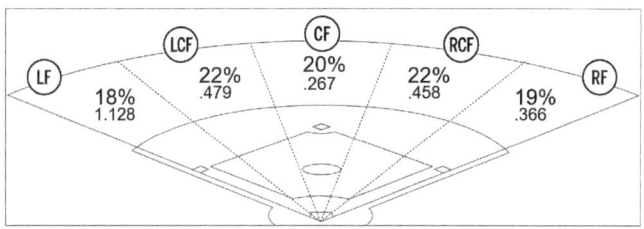

Strike Zone vs LHP　　　　　**Strike Zone vs RHP**

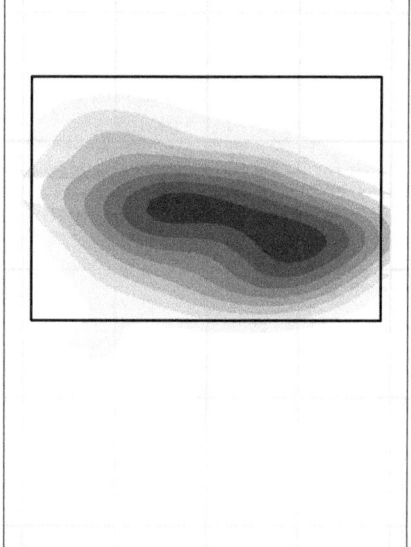

Adalberto Mondesi SS

Born: 07/27/95 Age: 25 Bats: S Throws: R
Height: 6'1" Weight: 200 Origin: International Free Agent, 2011

YEAR	TEAM	LVL	AGE	PA	R	2B	3B	HR	RBI	BB	K	SB	CS	AVG/OBP/SLG
2018	OMA	AAA	22	133	19	8	3	5	21	8	30	10	0	.250/.295/.492
2018	KC	MLB	22	291	47	13	3	14	37	11	77	32	7	.276/.306/.498
2019	OMA	AAA	23	37	5	1	1	1	3	4	13	2	1	.242/.324/.424
2019	KC	MLB	23	443	58	20	10	9	62	19	132	43	7	.263/.291/.424
2020	KC	MLB	24	233	33	11	3	6	22	11	70	24	8	.256/.294/.416
2021 FS	KC	MLB	25	600	66	24	9	16	66	31	186	37	7	.237/.280/.405
2021 DC	KC	MLB	25	605	67	25	10	16	66	31	187	37	7	.237/.280/.405

Comparables: Tim Anderson, Chris Owings, Michael Young

You have eggs, butter and flour, the essential ingredients for a soufflé. But if you don't use them correctly, the soufflé falls and you set off smoke alarms as it chars in the oven. With power, speed and off-the-charts athleticism, Mondesi has the ingredients to be a superstar in this league. Injuries have held him back in the past, but he was finally healthy in an abbreviated 2020. It was supposed to be the year where everything came together … but the season was one fallen soufflé after another. He whiffed in 30 percent of his plate appearances, made contact on just over 73 percent of his swings on pitches in the zone and led the league in caught stealing. What's the baking equivalent of seeing a ton of breaking balls off the plate?

YEAR	TEAM	LVL	AGE	PA	DRC+	BABIP	BRR	FRAA	WARP
2018	OMA	AAA	22	133	74	.291	1.2	SS(18): 0.6, 2B(6): 0.8	0.2
2018	KC	MLB	22	291	104	.335	0.3	SS(61): 1.2, 2B(12): 0.9	1.6
2019	OMA	AAA	23	37	67	.368	0.5	SS(6): 0.1	0.0
2019	KC	MLB	23	443	75	.357	3.1	SS(100): 6.3	1.6
2020	KC	MLB	24	233	60	.350	-0.3	SS(59): 2.9	-0.3
2021 FS	KC	MLB	25	600	85	.323	4.7	SS 2, 2B 0	1.3
2021 DC	KC	MLB	25	605	85	.323	4.8	SS 2	1.3

Adalberto Mondesi, continued

Batted Ball Distribution

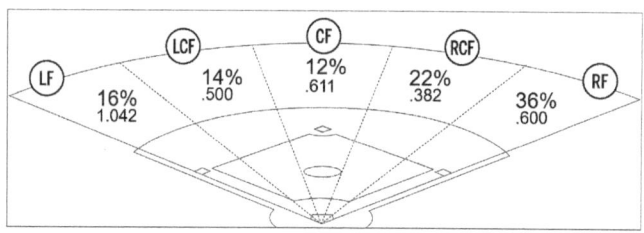

Strike Zone vs LHP

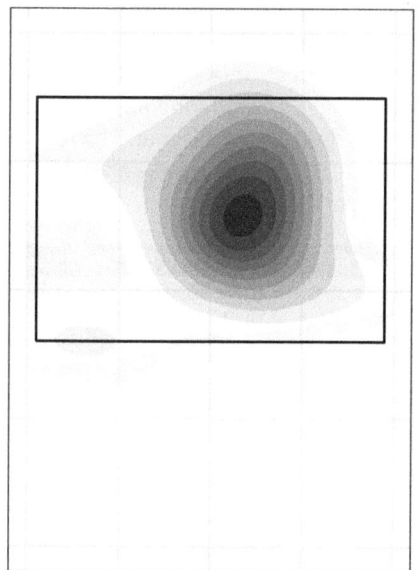

Strike Zone vs RHP

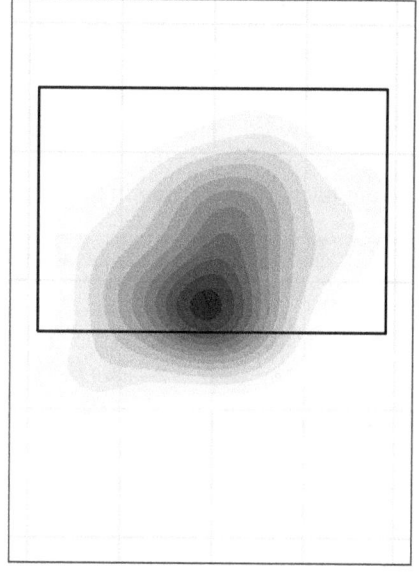

Kansas City Royals 2021

Ryan O'Hearn 1B
Born: 07/26/93   Age: 27   Bats: L   Throws: L
Height: 6'3"   Weight: 220   Origin: Round 8, 2014 Draft (#243 overall)

YEAR	TEAM	LVL	AGE	PA	R	2B	3B	HR	RBI	BB	K	SB	CS	AVG/OBP/SLG
2018	OMA	AAA	24	406	47	21	1	11	52	45	97	2	0	.232/.322/.391
2018	KC	MLB	24	170	23	10	2	12	30	20	45	0	0	.262/.353/.597
2019	OMA	AAA	25	149	20	10	1	9	28	17	31	0	0	.295/.383/.597
2019	KC	MLB	25	370	32	13	1	14	38	39	99	0	1	.195/.281/.369
2020	KC	MLB	26	132	7	6	0	2	18	18	37	0	0	.195/.303/.301
2021 FS	KC	MLB	27	600	66	26	2	20	68	65	182	0	1	.215/.305/.390
2021 DC	KC	MLB	27	96	10	4	0	3	10	10	29	0	0	.215/.305/.390

Comparables: Nick Esasky, Tommy Medica, Derrek Lee

O'Hearn was limited to just 12 plate appearances against left-handed pitching as part of a "soft" platoon at first base. (That sounds like a real platoon to us.) He actually held his own against same siders in 2020, small sample be damned. It was with the alleged platoon advantage where things fell apart. He upped his line drive rate which should have helped his offensive fortunes, but he continues to struggle mightily against off-speed stuff and can't hit a curve. His power took another hit for the second consecutive season. Relegated to both pinch and designated hitting in September, he closed out a forgettable season with three hits over his final 46 plate appearances. (Which has us wondering how we can remove the word "hitter" from pinch hitter and designated hitter and have it make sense.) Those successful 44 games from 2018 are looking like an outlier and are further and further in the rearview mirror.

YEAR	TEAM	LVL	AGE	PA	DRC+	BABIP	BRR	FRAA	WARP
2018	OMA	AAA	24	406	90	.286	3.9	1B(69): -6.3, LF(13): -2.1	-0.8
2018	KC	MLB	24	170	129	.293	-3.6	1B(31): 0.4, LF(1): -0.1	0.5
2019	OMA	AAA	25	149	129	.322	0.5	1B(25): 0.0	0.8
2019	KC	MLB	25	370	79	.230	-1.0	1B(94): -5.0, LF(2): -0.1	-1.0
2020	KC	MLB	26	132	83	.267	-0.7	1B(27): -0.3	-0.1
2021 FS	KC	MLB	27	600	91	.286	-0.8	1B -1, LF 0	0.1
2021 DC	KC	MLB	27	96	91	.286	-0.1	1B 0	0.0

Ryan O'Hearn, continued

Batted Ball Distribution

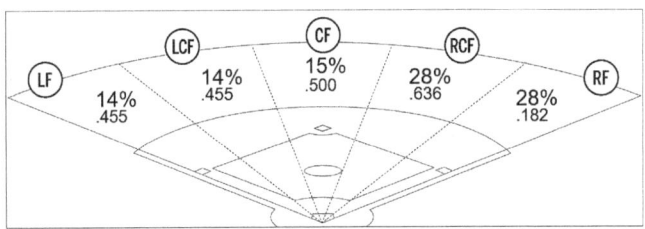

Strike Zone vs LHP

Strike Zone vs RHP

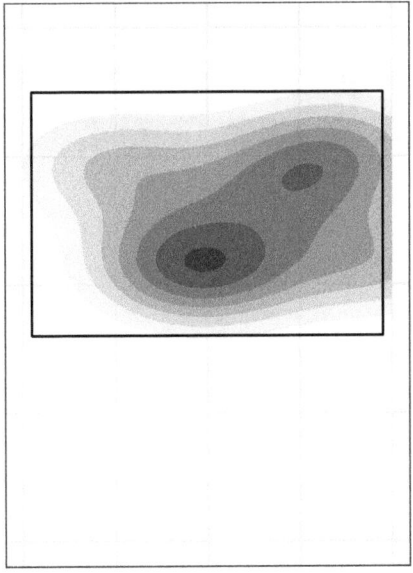
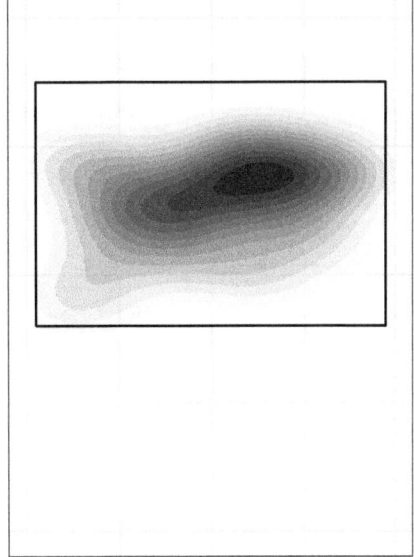

Edward Olivares OF

Born: 03/06/96   Age: 25   Bats: R   Throws: R
Height: 6'2"   Weight: 188   Origin: International Free Agent, 2014

YEAR	TEAM	LVL	AGE	PA	R	2B	3B	HR	RBI	BB	K	SB	CS	AVG/OBP/SLG
2018	LE	HI-A	22	575	79	25	10	12	62	29	102	21	8	.277/.321/.429
2019	AMA	AA	23	551	85	25	2	18	77	43	98	35	10	.283/.349/.453
2020	SD	MLB	24	36	4	1	0	1	3	2	14	0	1	.176/.222/.294
2020	KC	MLB	24	65	5	1	1	2	7	2	11	0	1	.274/.292/.419
2021 FS	KC	MLB	25	600	64	21	5	16	66	38	156	13	6	.230/.291/.382
2021 DC	KC	MLB	25	338	36	12	3	9	37	21	88	7	3	.230/.291/.382

Comparables: Nomar Mazara, Johnny Field, Billy McKinney

When the Royals acquired Franchy Cordero in July, conventional wisdom at the time believed the Padres made the move in part to create an opportunity for Olivares in their outfield. Then Olivares was dealt to Kansas City at the trade deadline in August. Baseball is weird that way. Still, following the retirement of Alex Gordon and a perpetual revolving door in center, the Royals are on the hunt for outfielders. Olivares brings a developing power profile, plus speed and can certainly hold his own in the expansive Kauffman Stadium outfield. There are some fourth outfielder rumblings around him, but the Royals can afford to provide him with an opportunity to see if he can exceed those expectations.

YEAR	TEAM	LVL	AGE	PA	DRC+	BABIP	BRR	FRAA	WARP
2018	LE	HI-A	22	575	103	.319	2.8	CF(115): 0.6, RF(7): 0.5, LF(4): 1.9	1.1
2019	AMA	AA	23	551	113	.317	3.7	RF(105): 5.5, CF(19): -0.1	2.9
2020	SD	MLB	24	36	67	.263	-0.3	LF(7): 0.1, RF(6): -0.1, CF(1): 0.0	-0.1
2020	KC	MLB	24	65	69	.300	-0.2	CF(10): -0.2, LF(7): 0.2, RF(5): 0.3	-0.1
2021 FS	KC	MLB	25	600	86	.289	1.5	RF 5, LF 4	1.6
2021 DC	KC	MLB	25	338	86	.289	0.9	RF 3, LF 2	0.7

Edward Olivares, continued

Batted Ball Distribution

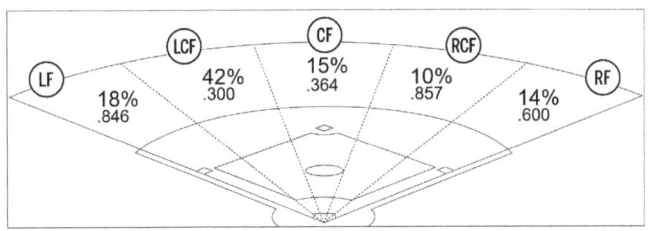

Strike Zone vs LHP   **Strike Zone vs RHP**

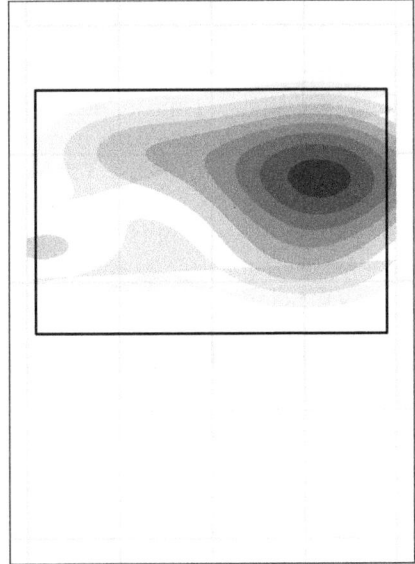 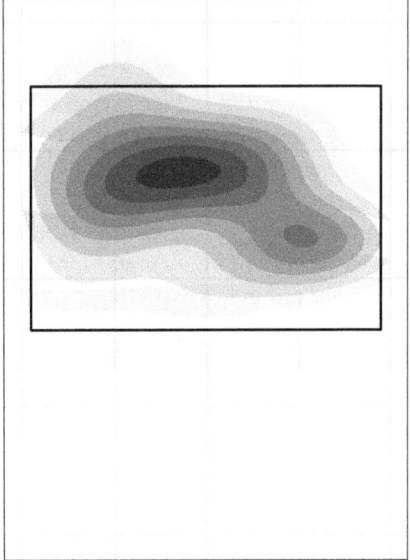

Kansas City Royals 2021

Salvador Perez C

Born: 05/10/90 Age: 31 Bats: R Throws: R
Height: 6'3" Weight: 250 Origin: International Free Agent, 2006

YEAR	TEAM	LVL	AGE	PA	R	2B	3B	HR	RBI	BB	K	SB	CS	AVG/OBP/SLG
2018	KC	MLB	28	544	52	23	0	27	80	17	108	1	1	.235/.274/.439
2020	KC	MLB	30	156	22	12	0	11	32	3	36	1	0	.333/.353/.633
2021 FS	KC	MLB	31	600	75	27	1	29	92	22	137	0	1	.252/.288/.465
2021 DC	KC	MLB	31	541	68	24	1	26	83	20	123	0	1	.252/.288/.465

Comparables: Wilson Ramos, Javy Lopez, Ivan Rodriguez

DRC+ has been kinder to Perez than almost any other offensive metric, but even then he's hovered around league-average for many of the last several seasons. Maybe the fact that he caught over 5,300 innings from 2014 to 2018—second to Yadier Molina, but

YEAR	TEAM	P. COUNT	FRM RUNS	BLK RUNS	THRW RUNS	TOT RUNS
2018	KC	14217	-9.9	-0.6	0.8	-9.7
2020	KC	4651	1.6	-0.1	-0.1	1.5
2021	KC	18038	-7.7	1.5	0.6	-5.7
2021	KC	18038	-7.7	-0.4	0.6	-7.6

over 300 more than third-place Jon Lucroy) had something to do with that. A year away from catching while rehabbing from Tommy John surgery, along with a rigorous offseason hitting program with Royals' special assignment hitting coach Mike Tosar resulted in his best offensive performance of his career. Between a bout of COVID-19 and blurred vision that sidelined him in the middle of the season, he ripped the ball consistently, with a hard-hit rate of 47 percent. Defensively, he even improved his framing, posting a positive CSAA for the first time since 2013. And the surgically repaired arm? Good as new it would appear. He gunned down 27 percent of would-be thieves. You never want to miss a year due to injury, but he's a testament to the benefits of what a year away can do when you put in the work to get back to where you belong.

YEAR	TEAM	LVL	AGE	PA	DRC+	BABIP	BRR	FRAA	WARP
2018	KC	MLB	28	544	103	.245	-3.7	C(96): -8.1, 1B(3): 0.0	1.3
2020	KC	MLB	30	156	135	.375	-1.2	C(34): -0.7, 1B(3): -0.3	1.1
2021 FS	KC	MLB	31	600	107	.279	-0.8	C -4, 1B 0	2.4
2021 DC	KC	MLB	31	541	107	.279	-0.7	C -5	2.0

Salvador Perez, continued

Batted Ball Distribution

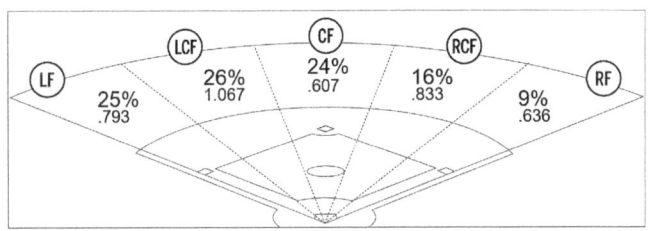

Strike Zone vs LHP   Strike Zone vs RHP

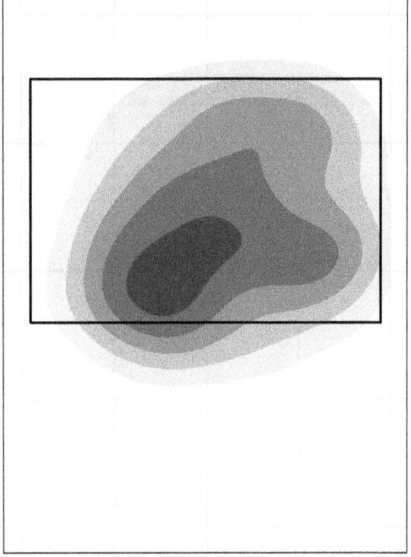

Carlos Santana 1B

Born: 04/08/86 Age: 35 Bats: S Throws: R
Height: 5'11" Weight: 210 Origin: International Free Agent, 2004

YEAR	TEAM	LVL	AGE	PA	R	2B	3B	HR	RBI	BB	K	SB	CS	AVG/OBP/SLG
2018	PHI	MLB	32	679	82	28	2	24	86	110	93	2	1	.229/.352/.414
2019	CLE	MLB	33	686	110	30	1	34	93	108	108	4	0	.281/.397/.515
2020	CLE	MLB	34	255	34	7	0	8	30	47	43	0	0	.199/.349/.350
2021 FS	KC	MLB	35	600	78	23	1	20	73	98	111	3	2	.231/.359/.410
2021 DC	KC	MLB	35	594	77	23	1	20	73	97	110	3	2	.231/.359/.410

Comparables: Kevin Youkilis, Boog Powell, Don Mincher

Santana's offensive potency and consistency are often taken for granted. To wit, did you know that last season was the first time in his career he finished with an OPS+ below 100? It's true. In Santana's first 10 seasons, he was reliably average or better in every single one of them. The good news is that he retained his impeccable eye at the plate and made a lot of hard outs, suggesting there's still some magic left in his stick. The bad news is that his timing couldn't have been worse: not only did Cleveland turn down his $17.5 million option, but they did so just months away from his 35th birthday. Santana will attempt to get back to being old steady before he's deemed too old to receive steady burn.

YEAR	TEAM	LVL	AGE	PA	DRC+	BABIP	BRR	FRAA	WARP
2018	PHI	MLB	32	679	108	.231	0.2	1B(149): -0.7, 3B(19): 0.6	1.8
2019	CLE	MLB	33	686	137	.293	1.1	1B(135): 3.9	4.8
2020	CLE	MLB	34	255	108	.212	1.4	1B(60): -4.2	0.2
2021 FS	KC	MLB	35	600	119	.255	-0.5	1B 0, 3B 0	2.3
2021 DC	KC	MLB	35	594	119	.255	-0.5	1B 0	2.2

Carlos Santana, continued

Batted Ball Distribution

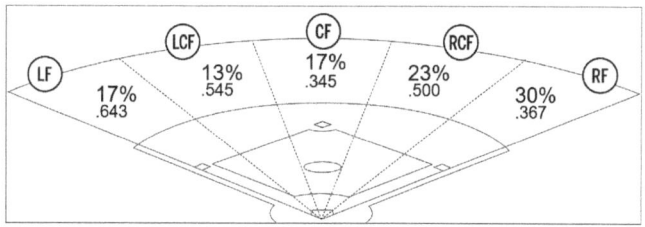

Strike Zone vs LHP

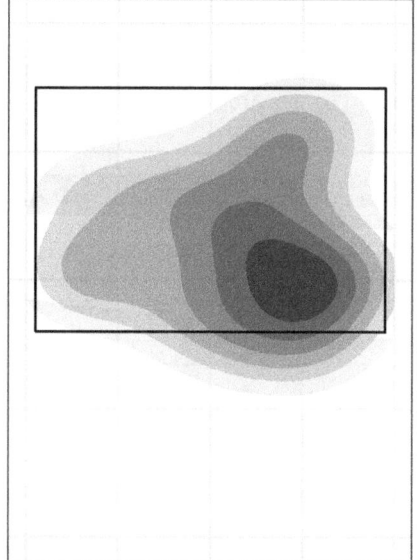

Strike Zone vs RHP

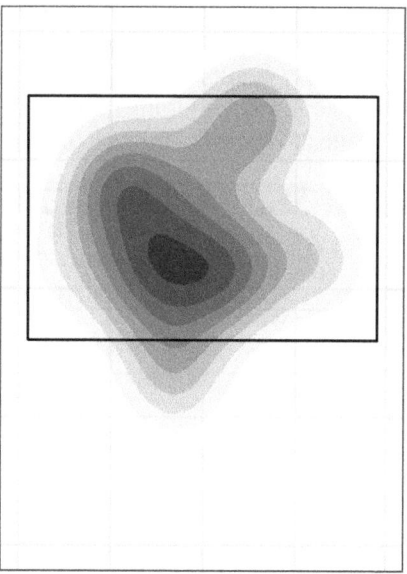

Jorge Soler RF

Born: 02/25/92 Age: 29 Bats: R Throws: R
Height: 6'4" Weight: 235 Origin: International Free Agent, 2012

YEAR	TEAM	LVL	AGE	PA	R	2B	3B	HR	RBI	BB	K	SB	CS	AVG/OBP/SLG
2018	KC	MLB	26	257	27	18	0	9	28	28	69	3	1	.265/.354/.466
2019	KC	MLB	27	679	95	33	1	48	117	73	178	3	1	.265/.354/.569
2020	KC	MLB	28	174	17	8	0	8	24	19	60	0	0	.228/.326/.443
2021 FS	KC	MLB	29	600	84	24	1	29	81	71	195	2	1	.231/.330/.456
2021 DC	KC	MLB	29	615	86	25	1	30	84	72	200	2	1	.231/.330/.456

Comparables: Jay Buhner, Jeremy Hermida, Jay Bruce

Baseball can be cruel. Once you think you have this game licked, it can turn on you in an instant. One year removed from playing in every game and setting the Royals' single-season home run record, Soler was once again bitten by the injury bug and saw his power output decline precipitously. The nadir of his season came not when he landed on the IL for an oblique strain, but rather in a five-game stretch in mid-August where he struck out 15 times in 19 plate appearances. The Soler Power may have dimmed in 2020, but with an average exit velocity and hard-hit rate both in the 93rd percentile of all hitters, it's still glimmering. He just needs to rediscover how to tap into that power to get the same kind of results he saw in the prior year. Perhaps another offseason of work with Mike Tosar, the hitting guru who turned his career around with sessions in 2017 and 2018 can flip the switch. Shine on.

YEAR	TEAM	LVL	AGE	PA	DRC+	BABIP	BRR	FRAA	WARP
2018	KC	MLB	26	257	100	.340	-0.5	RF(52): -1.0	0.4
2019	KC	MLB	27	679	141	.294	-4.3	RF(56): 0.4	4.5
2020	KC	MLB	28	174	91	.317	-0.5	RF(8): -0.7	0.0
2021 FS	KC	MLB	29	600	121	.302	-0.7	RF 0	2.8
2021 DC	KC	MLB	29	615	121	.302	-0.7	RF 0	2.6

Jorge Soler, continued

Batted Ball Distribution

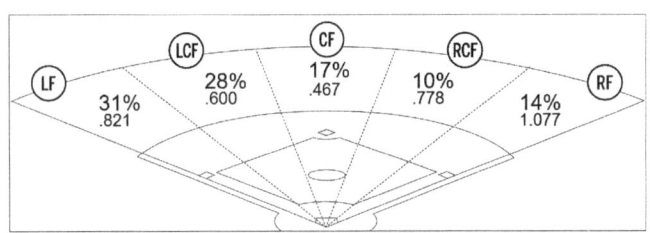

Strike Zone vs LHP   Strike Zone vs RHP

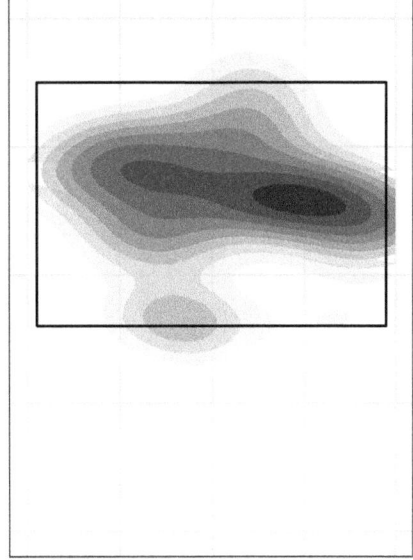

Michael A. Taylor CF

Born: 03/26/91   Age: 30   Bats: R   Throws: R
Height: 6'4"   Weight: 215   Origin: Round 6, 2009 Draft (#172 overall)

YEAR	TEAM	LVL	AGE	PA	R	2B	3B	HR	RBI	BB	K	SB	CS	AVG/OBP/SLG
2018	WAS	MLB	27	385	46	22	3	6	28	29	116	24	6	.227/.287/.357
2019	HBG	AA	28	247	36	16	2	9	35	25	69	10	6	.248/.324/.463
2019	WAS	MLB	28	97	10	7	0	1	3	7	34	6	0	.250/.305/.364
2020	WAS	MLB	29	99	11	6	0	5	16	6	27	0	0	.196/.253/.424
2021 FS	KC	MLB	30	600	64	24	2	16	62	46	194	23	8	.212/.275/.358
2021 DC	KC	MLB	30	397	42	16	1	10	41	30	128	16	5	.212/.275/.358

Comparables: Kirk Nieuwenhuis, Laynce Nix, Drew Stubbs

The Royals, seemingly more than any other team in baseball, have a thing for speedy, no-hit outfielders. Taylor, who joined Kansas City after being released by the Nationals, is the latest in a long line (though he probably won't be the last). The upside here is that he's moved in a small deadline deal and ends up part of a classic World Series moment. Shy of that, he's going to be changing teams frequently as he enters his final year before qualifying for free agency.

YEAR	TEAM	LVL	AGE	PA	DRC+	BABIP	BRR	FRAA	WARP
2018	WAS	MLB	27	385	66	.320	1.3	CF(113): 8.9, 1B(1): -0.0	0.8
2019	HBG	AA	28	247	121	.315	3.9	CF(43): -1.2, RF(6): -0.1	1.5
2019	WAS	MLB	28	97	57	.396	-0.6	CF(25): -0.0, RF(7): -0.8	-0.3
2020	WAS	MLB	29	99	88	.217	-0.5	LF(14): 2.3, CF(11): 0.0, RF(11): 0.2	0.2
2021 FS	KC	MLB	30	600	74	.292	2.3	CF 4, 1B 0	0.5
2021 DC	KC	MLB	30	397	74	.292	1.5	CF 3	0.4

Michael A. Taylor, continued

Batted Ball Distribution

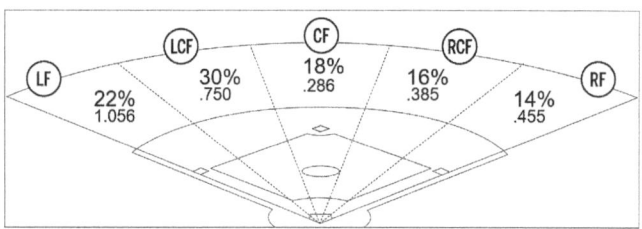

Strike Zone vs LHP   Strike Zone vs RHP

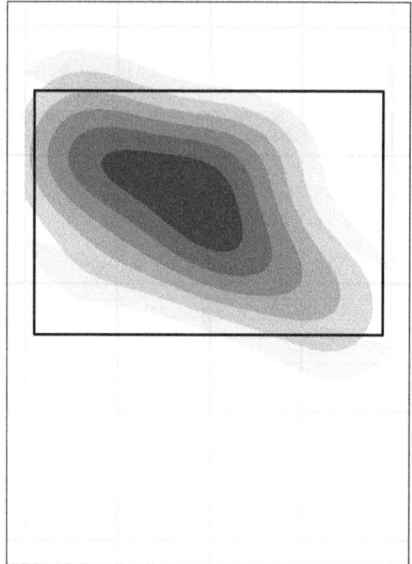

Scott Barlow RHP

Born: 12/18/92 Age: 28 Bats: R Throws: R
Height: 6'3" Weight: 215 Origin: Round 6, 2011 Draft (#194 overall)

YEAR	TEAM	LVL	AGE	W	L	SV	G	GS	IP	H	HR	BB/9	K/9	K	GB%	BABIP
2018	OMA	AAA	25	1	4	1	13	10	45^2	54	9	4.1	9.9	50	36.3%	.360
2018	KC	MLB	25	1	1	0	6	0	15	16	2	1.8	9.0	15	40.4%	.311
2019	OMA	AAA	26	0	0	1	3	0	6	3	0	4.5	7.5	5	21.4%	.214
2019	KC	MLB	26	3	3	1	61	0	70^1	64	6	4.7	11.8	92	39.3%	.341
2020	KC	MLB	27	2	1	2	32	0	30	27	4	2.7	11.7	39	45.3%	.324
2021 FS	KC	MLB	28	2	2	1	57	0	50	42	5	4.1	10.6	59	41.2%	.295
2021 DC	KC	MLB	28	2	2	1	57	0	61	52	7	4.1	10.6	72	41.2%	.295

Comparables: Michael Feliz, Clay Holmes, Erick Fedde

Barlow entered manager Mike Matheny's Circle of Bullpen Trust and never left, racking up a major league-leading 32 appearances. Using the tired-but-true reliever formula of heaters up and breakers down, his slider remained his knockout pitch, garnering a breezy 42 percent whiff rate and a .217 batting average against. A minor-league free agent from the Dodgers organization whom the Royals penned to a split contract and awarded a spot on the 40-man roster before he ever tossed a big-league inning, he represents exactly the type of player the small-market Royals need to grab when assembling a bullpen.

YEAR	TEAM	LVL	AGE	WHIP	ERA	DRA-	WARP	MPH	FB%	WHF	CSP
2018	OMA	AAA	25	1.64	6.11	77	1.0				
2018	KC	MLB	25	1.27	3.60	82	0.2	92.9	53.0%	24.1%	
2019	OMA	AAA	26	1.00	0.00	82	0.1				
2019	KC	MLB	26	1.44	4.22	86	0.9	96.3	43.0%	33.8%	
2020	KC	MLB	27	1.20	4.20	75	0.7	96.6	37.3%	37.6%	
2021 FS	KC	MLB	28	1.30	3.76	89	0.6	96.3	41.5%	34.6%	44.0%
2021 DC	KC	MLB	28	1.30	3.76	89	0.7	96.3	41.5%	34.6%	44.0%

Scott Barlow, continued

Pitch Shape vs LHH

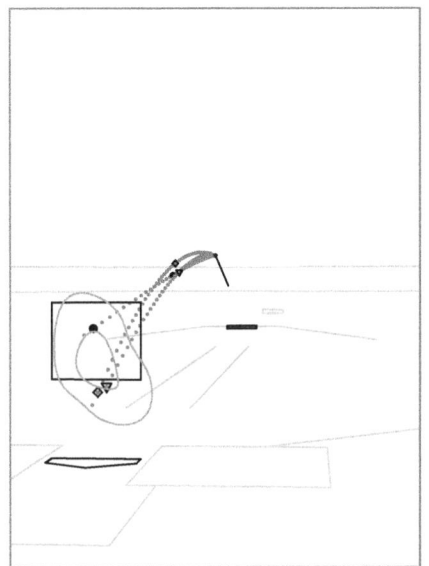

Pitch Shape vs RHH

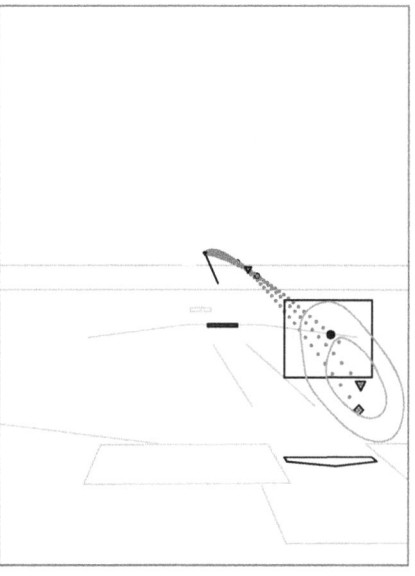

Type	Frequency	Velocity	H Movement	V Movement
● Fastball	36.8%	95.1 [108]	-5.4 [106]	-13.4 [105]
▽ Slider	41.3%	83.6 [98]	6.9 [106]	-36.5 [92]
◇ Curveball	20.7%	78.3 [99]	13.4 [124]	-49.6 [97]

Kris Bubic LHP

Born: 08/19/97   Age: 23   Bats: L   Throws: L
Height: 6'3"   Weight: 220   Origin: Round 1, 2018 Draft (#40 overall)

YEAR	TEAM	LVL	AGE	W	L	SV	G	GS	IP	H	HR	BB/9	K/9	K	GB%	BABIP
2018	IDF	ROK	20	2	3	0	10	10	38	38	2	4.5	12.6	53	41.2%	.379
2019	LEX	LO-A	21	4	1	0	9	9	47^2	27	3	2.8	14.2	75	44.6%	.273
2019	WIL	HI-A	21	7	4	0	17	17	101^2	76	3	2.4	9.7	110	41.4%	.299
2020	KC	MLB	22	1	6	0	10	10	50	52	8	4.0	8.8	49	45.0%	.312
2021 FS	KC	MLB	23	9	8	0	26	26	150	139	18	4.4	9.5	158	44.6%	.300
2021 DC	KC	MLB	23	7	7	0	24	24	121.3	113	15	4.4	9.5	128	44.6%	.300

Comparables: Trevor Rogers, Patrick Sandoval, Brock Burke

Given his repeatable mechanics and a consistent arm slot, it wasn't a surprise that Bubic, the youngest of the baby Royals starting pitching prospect quartet, made his way to the majors in 2020. That arm slot repetition comes in handy because Bubic sports a 12 mph separation between his heater and his change, inducing awkward swings from many a batter. It was the development of a wipeout curve, though, that truly accelerated his timeline to The Show. He threw the yakker over 15 percent of the time and surrendered only four base hits—all singles—with the majority of the curveballs put in play finding their way to webbing of his infielder's mitts. That's a tidy .174 BAA on the pitch, in case you were wondering. He's the first pitcher in franchise history to make the jump from A-ball to the majors and with that successful third pitch, it stands to reason he'll be making his home in the Kansas City rotation for years to come.

YEAR	TEAM	LVL	AGE	WHIP	ERA	DRA-	WARP	MPH	FB%	WHF	CSP
2018	IDF	ROK	20	1.50	4.03						
2019	LEX	LO-A	21	0.88	2.08	49	1.6				
2019	WIL	HI-A	21	1.01	2.30	72	1.9				
2020	KC	MLB	22	1.48	4.32	110	0.2	94.1	54.2%	24.9%	
2021 FS	KC	MLB	23	1.42	4.39	101	1.3	94.1	54.2%	24.9%	48.3%
2021 DC	KC	MLB	23	1.42	4.39	101	1.1	94.1	54.2%	24.9%	48.3%

Kris Bubic, continued

Pitch Shape vs LHH

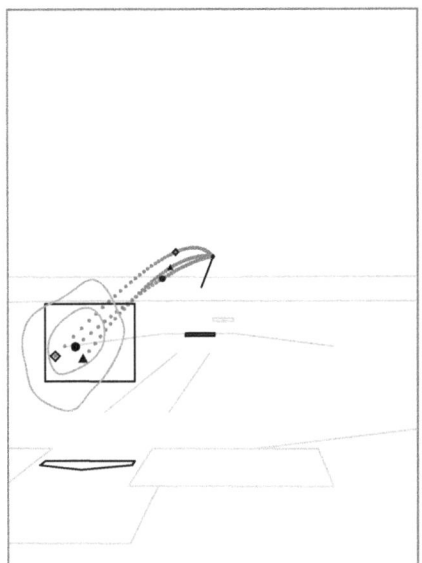

Pitch Shape vs RHH

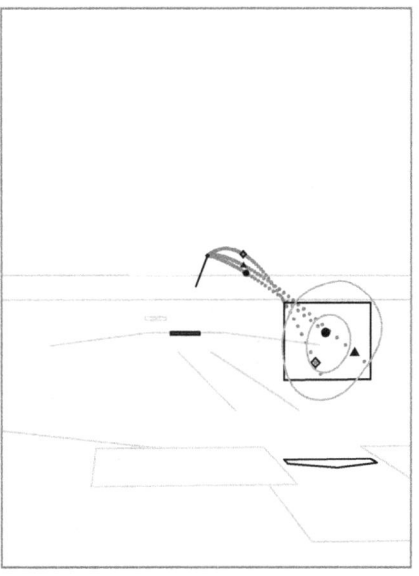

Type	Frequency	Velocity	H Movement	V Movement
● Fastball	54.0%	91.7 [97]	5.3 [107]	-14.6 [102]
▲ Changeup	29.7%	79.9 [79]	11.2 [103]	-29.2 [95]
◇ Curveball	15.8%	78.7 [100]	-9 [106]	-50.4 [95]

Danny Duffy   LHP

Born: 12/21/88   Age: 32   Bats: L   Throws: L
Height: 6'3"   Weight: 185   Origin: Round 3, 2007 Draft (#96 overall)

YEAR	TEAM	LVL	AGE	W	L	SV	G	GS	IP	H	HR	BB/9	K/9	K	GB%	BABIP
2018	KC	MLB	29	8	12	0	28	28	155	161	23	4.1	8.2	141	35.2%	.305
2019	NWA	AA	30	1	0	0	2	2	10^1	8	1	0.0	9.6	11	46.2%	.280
2019	KC	MLB	30	7	6	0	23	23	130^2	125	21	3.2	7.9	115	35.0%	.285
2020	KC	MLB	31	4	4	0	12	11	56^1	53	10	3.5	9.1	57	31.7%	.287
2021 FS	KC	MLB	32	9	9	0	26	26	150	145	25	3.5	8.8	146	34.4%	.290
2021 DC	KC	MLB	32	8	8	0	25	25	139.7	135	23	3.5	8.8	136	34.4%	.290

Comparables: Jhoulys Chacín, Trevor Cahill, Brett Anderson

With a rotation of prospects on the horizon, Duffy, a pitching staff mainstay since 2011, has unlocked grizzled veteran status. He's been an averageish starter the last three seasons while navigating sundry injuries. The Royals handled him with care in 2020, rarely letting him pass 90 pitches; he averaged just 14 outs per start. He's been a rumored trade candidate in the past, but with one year remaining on an extension signed prior to the 2017 season, his trade value is well past its peak. Perhaps manager Mike Matheny tipped his hand for 2021 when he used the lefty out of the bullpen for his final appearance of 2020. He's experienced success there in the past, and with all those young arms lining up for rotation innings, that may be the best location for the Duffman to finish out his Royals career.

YEAR	TEAM	LVL	AGE	WHIP	ERA	DRA-	WARP	MPH	FB%	WHF	CSP
2018	KC	MLB	29	1.49	4.88	123	-0.4	95.5	55.8%	23.4%	
2019	NWA	AA	30	0.77	0.87	66	0.2				
2019	KC	MLB	30	1.31	4.34	109	0.6	94.5	53.0%	24.2%	
2020	KC	MLB	31	1.33	4.95	129	-0.4	94.4	53.4%	25.6%	
2021 FS	KC	MLB	32	1.36	4.51	106	1.0	94.8	53.9%	24.4%	49.8%
2021 DC	KC	MLB	32	1.36	4.51	106	0.9	94.8	53.9%	24.4%	49.8%

Danny Duffy, continued

Pitch Shape vs LHH

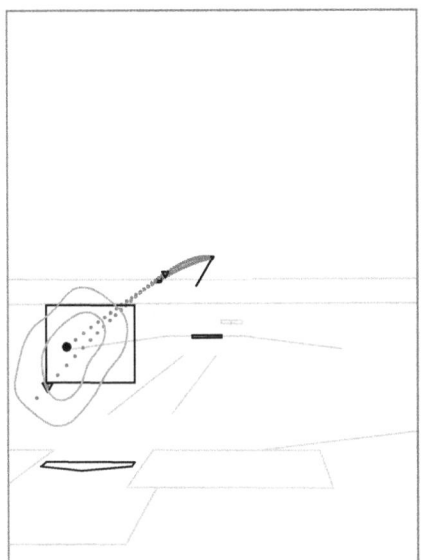

Pitch Shape vs RHH

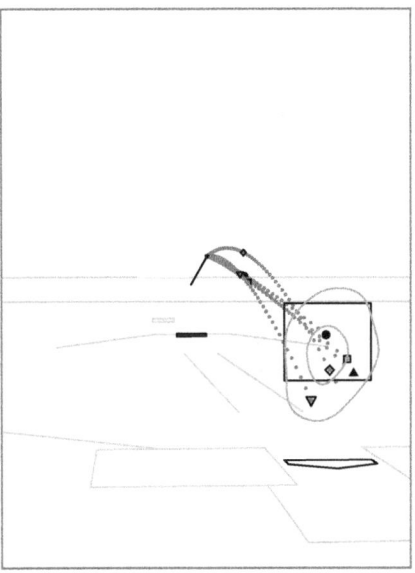

Type	Frequency	Velocity	H Movement	V Movement
● Fastball	39.0%	92.4 [100]	5.3 [107]	-12.3 [108]
□ Sinker	14.4%	92.2 [99]	10.9 [116]	-15.7 [116]
▲ Changeup	15.3%	84.1 [96]	12.6 [95]	-24.7 [108]
▽ Slider	17.2%	82.8 [95]	-4.4 [97]	-36.7 [91]
◇ Curveball	14.1%	75.7 [89]	-7.2 [98]	-54.6 [86]

Kansas City Royals 2021

Jesse Hahn RHP
Born: 07/30/89   Age: 31   Bats: R   Throws: R
Height: 6'5"   Weight: 210   Origin: Round 6, 2010 Draft (#191 overall)

YEAR	TEAM	LVL	AGE	W	L	SV	G	GS	IP	H	HR	BB/9	K/9	K	GB%	BABIP
2019	KC	MLB	29	0	1	0	6	0	4²	7	1	11.6	13.5	7	42.9%	.462
2020	KC	MLB	30	1	0	3	18	0	17¹	4	0	4.2	9.9	19	45.9%	.108
2021 FS	KC	MLB	31	2	2	0	57	0	50	47	6	3.9	8.8	48	45.4%	.294
2021 DC	KC	MLB	31	2	2	0	57	0	61	57	7	3.9	8.8	59	45.4%	.294

Comparables: Trevor Cahill, Jhoulys Chacín, Dan Straily

You never want to hear the words "a second Tommy John surgery" from the doctor examining your MRI. After undergoing a TJ operation in 2010, and after injuring his elbow after just a handful of Cactus League innings, Hahn wasn't looking forward to another arduous rehab process. Instead, he underwent a repair procedure similar to the one Seth Maness had a couple of years prior, where the torn tendon was reinforced with strong sutures. It worked. At full health and pitching in relief, Hahn went mostly with a sinker/curve combo and it was lethal. Opponents hit just .088 against a two-seamer that averaged 95 mph. And of the 20 plate appearances that ended on his curve, not a single ball dropped for a base hit. By the last week of the season, he was closing games. As the Royals continue their quest to build a better bullpen, he's in the mix to remain in the ninth-inning role.

YEAR	TEAM	LVL	AGE	WHIP	ERA	DRA-	WARP	MPH	FB%	WHF	CSP
2019	KC	MLB	29	2.79	13.50	115	0.0	96.5	62.6%	30.4%	
2020	KC	MLB	30	0.69	0.52	85	0.3	96.6	56.5%	24.2%	
2021 FS	KC	MLB	31	1.37	4.20	98	0.3	96.6	57.7%	25.4%	47.4%
2021 DC	KC	MLB	31	1.37	4.20	98	0.4	96.6	57.7%	25.4%	47.4%

Jesse Hahn, continued

Pitch Shape vs LHH

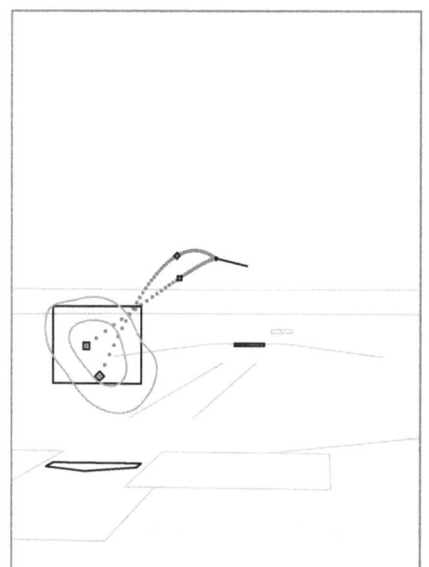

Pitch Shape vs RHH

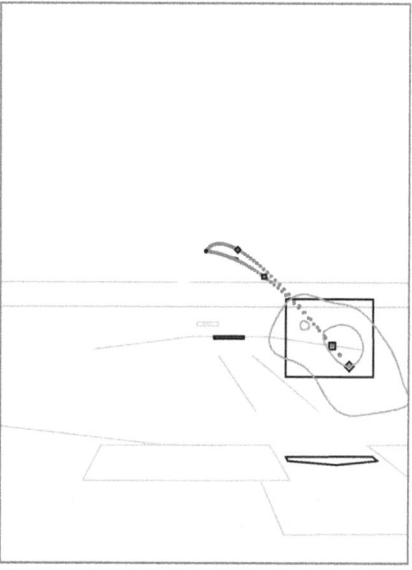

Type	Frequency	Velocity	H Movement	V Movement
☐ Sinker	55.8%	95.2 [114]	-14.4 [90]	-17.2 [111]
▽ Slider	9.2%	82.6 [94]	12.6 [128]	-42.4 [75]
◇ Curveball	34.2%	78.6 [100]	13.9 [126]	-54.1 [87]

Matt Harvey RHP

Born: 03/27/89 Age: 32 Bats: R Throws: R
Height: 6'4" Weight: 220 Origin: Round 1, 2010 Draft (#7 overall)

YEAR	TEAM	LVL	AGE	W	L	SV	G	GS	IP	H	HR	BB/9	K/9	K	GB%	BABIP
2018	CIN	MLB	29	7	7	0	24	24	128	132	21	2.0	7.8	111	43.4%	.299
2018	NYM	MLB	29	0	2	0	8	4	27	33	6	3.0	6.7	20	39.8%	.318
2019	LAA	MLB	30	3	5	0	12	12	59^2	63	13	4.4	5.9	39	43.1%	.276
2020	KC	MLB	31	0	3	0	7	4	11^2	27	6	3.9	7.7	10	42.0%	.477
2021 FS	KC	MLB	32	2	3	0	57	0	50	51	7	3.0	7.3	40	42.0%	.294

Comparables: Yovani Gallardo, Masahiro Tanaka, David Price

Given their situation as one of the smaller of the small market clubs, the Royals often have to take a stroll in the discount pitching aisle, looking for bargains as they shop for innings. Recent past purchases have included Clay Buchholz, Homer Bailey and now Harvey. The pitcher formerly known as the Dark Knight is still finding his way after injuries have diminished his heater and, more worryingly, robbed him of his command. Purchases in the discount pitching aisle come as-is, without the option of a refund. Sometimes it just doesn't work. But that won't stop the Royals from keeping their frequent shopper card up to date.

YEAR	TEAM	LVL	AGE	WHIP	ERA	DRA-	WARP	MPH	FB%	WHF	CSP
2018	CIN	MLB	29	1.25	4.50	107	0.7	96.3	58.7%	21.1%	
2018	NYM	MLB	29	1.56	7.00	93	0.3	94.3	61.2%	18.2%	
2019	LAA	MLB	30	1.54	7.09	156	-1.2	95.0	47.6%	22.1%	
2020	KC	MLB	31	2.74	11.57	128	-0.1	96.1	53.5%	17.5%	
2021 FS	KC	MLB	32	1.36	4.47	105	0.1	95.8	54.1%	20.7%	50.2%

Matt Harvey, continued

Pitch Shape vs LHH

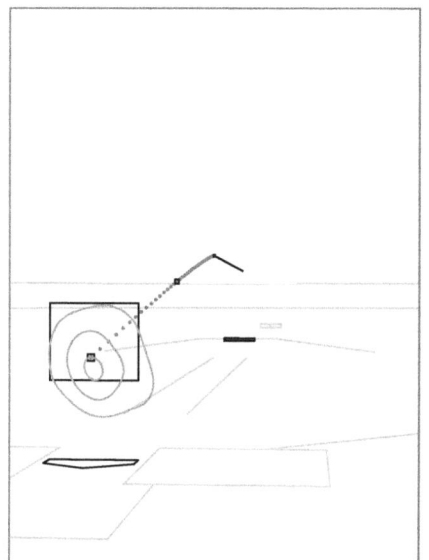

Pitch Shape vs RHH

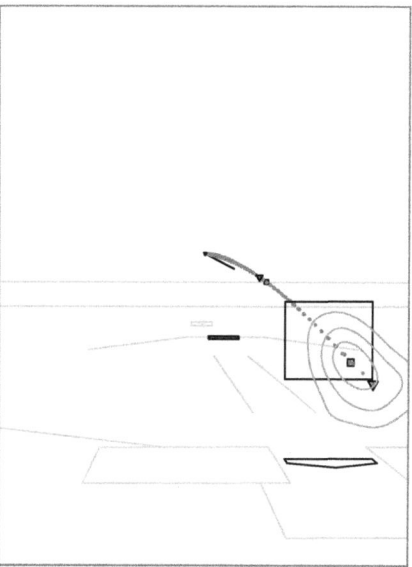

Type	Frequency	Velocity	H Movement	V Movement
● Fastball	12.7%	94.5 [106]	-9.1 [89]	-15.1 [100]
□ Sinker	40.8%	94.3 [110]	-11.8 [109]	-16.9 [112]
▲ Changeup	9.8%	85 [99]	-10.6 [106]	-24.8 [107]
▽ Slider	22.4%	87.3 [115]	2.4 [89]	-29 [114]
◇ Curveball	14.3%	82 [113]	3.2 [82]	-43.9 [110]

Carlos Hernández   RHP

Born: 03/11/97   Age: 24   Bats: R   Throws: R
Height: 6'4"   Weight: 250   Origin: International Free Agent, 2016

YEAR	TEAM	LVL	AGE	W	L	SV	G	GS	IP	H	HR	BB/9	K/9	K	GB%	BABIP
2018	LEX	LO-A	21	6	5	0	15	15	79^1	71	7	2.6	9.3	82	41.4%	.299
2019	ROY	ROK	22	0	2	0	5	5	11	14	1	2.5	9.8	12	41.2%	.394
2019	BUR	ROK+	22	0	0	0	3	3	10^2	11	1	10.1	11.0	13	33.3%	.345
2019	LEX	LO-A	22	3	3	0	7	7	36	34	5	2.2	10.8	43	37.2%	.326
2020	KC	MLB	23	0	1	0	5	3	14^2	19	4	3.7	8.0	13	42.6%	.349
2021 FS	KC	MLB	24	8	9	0	26	26	150	146	21	5.0	8.3	137	41.2%	.293
2021 DC	KC	MLB	24	4	5	0	16	16	71	69	10	5.0	8.3	65	41.2%	.293

Comparables: Luis Perdomo, Nick Neidert, Seranthony Domínguez

Every season, in every organization, there's a player who massively exceeds expectations. That player was Hernandez for Kansas City. Invited to the major-league camp in spring training, he was ultimately left out of the 60-man mix when teams reconvened for summer camp. But when the Royals had an opening, they called and the right-hander was ready. He made his big-league debut just a couple of weeks later. He features a mid-90s heater and an above-average curve to pair with a decent change. Signed as a 19-year-old out of Venezuela, he's shown adaptability at every stop on his journey, striking out over a batter per inning along the way. Even with the plethora of pitching prospects in the org, the Royals see him as a starter.

YEAR	TEAM	LVL	AGE	WHIP	ERA	DRA-	WARP	MPH	FB%	WHF	CSP
2018	LEX	LO-A	21	1.18	3.29	130	-0.9				
2019	ROY	ROK	22	1.55	7.36						
2019	BUR	ROK+	22	2.16	9.28						
2019	LEX	LO-A	22	1.19	3.50	86	0.4				
2020	KC	MLB	23	1.70	4.91	111	0.0	98.9	51.4%	25.4%	
2021 FS	KC	MLB	24	1.53	5.08	114	0.3	98.9	51.4%	25.4%	48.2%
2021 DC	KC	MLB	24	1.53	5.08	114	0.0	98.9	51.4%	25.4%	48.2%

Carlos Hernández, continued

Pitch Shape vs LHH

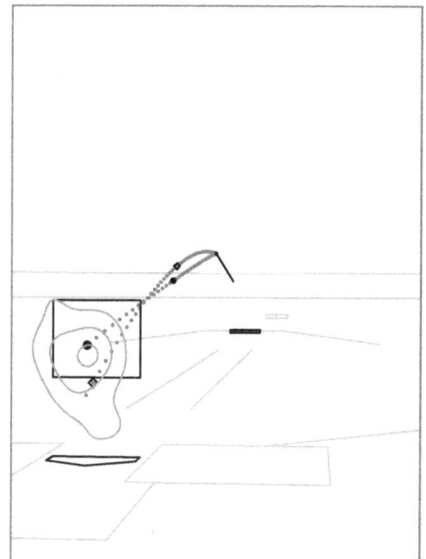

Pitch Shape vs RHH

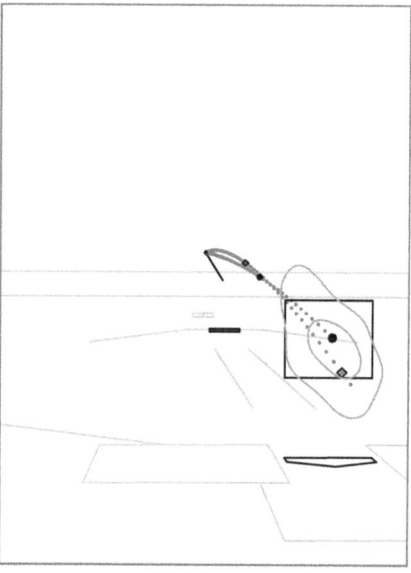

Type	Frequency	Velocity	H Movement	V Movement
● Fastball	51.4%	96.4 [112]	-8.6 [91]	-11.5 [110]
▲ Changeup	15.3%	86.1 [104]	-10.4 [107]	-23.6 [111]
◇ Curveball	33.3%	83.3 [118]	3.7 [84]	-41.7 [115]

Kansas City Royals 2021

Greg Holland RHP
Born: 11/20/85 Age: 35 Bats: R Throws: R
Height: 5'10" Weight: 205 Origin: Round 10, 2007 Draft (#306 overall)

YEAR	TEAM	LVL	AGE	W	L	SV	G	GS	IP	H	HR	BB/9	K/9	K	GB%	BABIP
2018	WAS	MLB	32	2	0	3	24	0	21^1	9	1	4.2	10.5	25	47.7%	.186
2018	STL	MLB	32	0	2	0	32	0	25	34	1	7.9	7.9	22	37.5%	.384
2019	HBG	AA	33	1	0	0	8	0	9	4	0	3.0	9.0	9	36.4%	.182
2019	ARI	MLB	33	1	2	17	40	0	35^2	25	5	6.1	10.3	41	44.8%	.244
2020	KC	MLB	34	3	0	6	28	0	28^1	20	1	2.2	9.8	31	50.7%	.275
2021 FS	KC	MLB	35	2	2	23	57	0	50	44	6	4.8	9.6	53	44.4%	.292
2021 DC	KC	MLB	35	2	2	23	57	0	61	54	7	4.8	9.6	64	44.4%	.292

Comparables: David Robertson, Francisco Rodríguez, Mark Melancon

"Clapton is god," read the graffiti in London just before the guitarist joined Cream, the trio that ultimately launched the supergroup era of rock. As closer, Holland filled a similar, leading role for the Royals' own super bullpen trio known as HDH while they hammered batters in 2014 & '15. Pitching on a shredded UCL for most of his final season for the Royals, The Dirty South went as long as he could before it finally gave out in the September stretch run. Since returning from that injury, he's pitched well in short bursts, so it wasn't exactly a surprise the 60-game season suited him well, and once again, with a heart full of soul, he found himself closing games for the Royals. No supergroups last forever, his bullpenmates have moved on and he's unplugged now, but still getting the job done.

YEAR	TEAM	LVL	AGE	WHIP	ERA	DRA-	WARP	MPH	FB%	WHF	CSP
2018	WAS	MLB	32	0.89	0.84	84	0.3	94.3	44.2%	37.1%	
2018	STL	MLB	32	2.24	7.92	151	-0.5	94.6	42.9%	27.2%	
2019	HBG	AA	33	0.78	0.00	70	0.1				
2019	ARI	MLB	33	1.37	4.54	91	0.3	93.7	47.3%	29.9%	
2020	KC	MLB	34	0.95	1.91	77	0.6	94.7	37.4%	30.0%	
2021 FS	KC	MLB	35	1.43	4.31	99	0.3	94.3	42.4%	30.2%	44.2%
2021 DC	KC	MLB	35	1.43	4.31	99	0.3	94.3	42.4%	30.2%	44.2%

Greg Holland, continued

Pitch Shape vs LHH

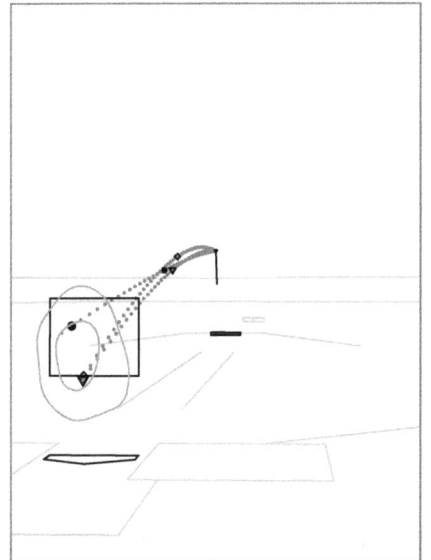

Pitch Shape vs RHH

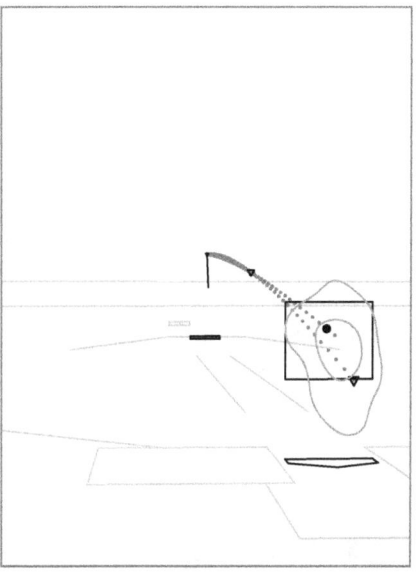

Type	Frequency	Velocity	H Movement	V Movement
● Fastball	37.0%	93.2 [102]	-0.5 [130]	-13.1 [106]
▽ Slider	50.1%	86.1 [110]	4.2 [96]	-31.8 [106]
◇ Curveball	11.5%	78.8 [101]	4.4 [87]	-45.7 [106]

Jakob Junis   RHP

Born: 09/16/92   Age: 28   Bats: R   Throws: R
Height: 6'3"   Weight: 220   Origin: Round 29, 2011 Draft (#876 overall)

YEAR	TEAM	LVL	AGE	W	L	SV	G	GS	IP	H	HR	BB/9	K/9	K	GB%	BABIP
2018	KC	MLB	25	9	12	0	30	30	177	182	32	2.2	8.3	164	41.8%	.300
2019	KC	MLB	26	9	14	0	31	31	175^1	192	31	3.0	8.4	164	43.0%	.318
2020	KC	MLB	27	0	2	0	8	6	25^1	35	7	2.1	6.8	19	46.0%	.350
2021 FS	KC	MLB	28	2	3	0	57	0	50	50	7	2.7	8.1	45	42.4%	.298
2021 DC	KC	MLB	28	2	2	0	51	0	55	56	8	2.7	8.1	49	42.4%	.298

Comparables: Daniel Mengden, Nick Pivetta, Dylan Bundy

It's a simple pitching philosophy: Hard stuff up, breaking stuff down. The Royals started preaching this in 2020 and Junis is one of the pitchers who embraced the evolution of organizational philosophy. But pitching, no matter the philosophy, is an unforgiving art. Miss the location by millimeters and punishment will follow. The right-hander lives on a slider/fastball combo and struggled to locate the former with consistency and got lit up on the latter when he wasn't able to elevate it enough. The sum of the parts were far too many tasty pitches in the fat part of the zone which led to some well-fed hitters. He finished the season in the bullpen and that figures to be his home long-term. Given his pitch combo it wouldn't be surprising to see him thrive in a relief role.

YEAR	TEAM	LVL	AGE	WHIP	ERA	DRA-	WARP	MPH	FB%	WHF	CSP
2018	KC	MLB	25	1.27	4.37	123	-0.4	93.0	53.3%	22.2%	
2019	KC	MLB	26	1.43	5.24	121	-0.3	93.3	50.8%	22.6%	
2020	KC	MLB	27	1.62	6.39	118	0.0	93.4	49.2%	20.5%	
2021 FS	KC	MLB	28	1.32	4.47	105	0.1	93.3	51.3%	22.3%	48.5%
2021 DC	KC	MLB	28	1.32	4.47	105	0.3	93.3	51.3%	22.3%	48.5%

Jakob Junis, continued

Pitch Shape vs LHH

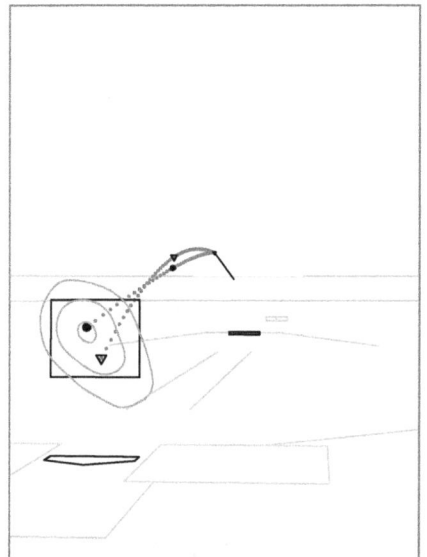

Pitch Shape vs RHH

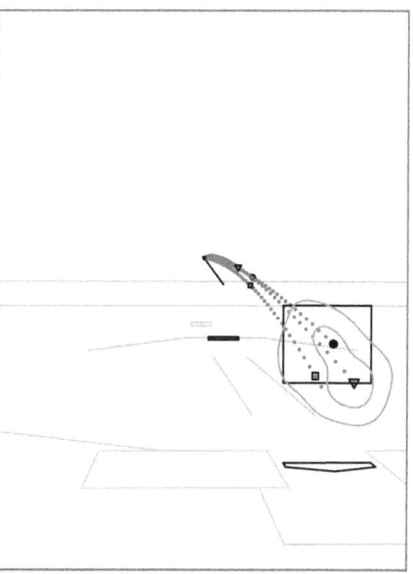

Type	Frequency	Velocity	H Movement	V Movement
● Fastball	34.4%	91.4 [96]	-4 [113]	-16.5 [96]
☐ Sinker	14.7%	90.8 [92]	-10.5 [119]	-21.6 [96]
▲ Changeup	4.6%	84.7 [98]	-9.1 [114]	-28.7 [97]
▽ Slider	46.1%	80.3 [84]	14.4 [135]	-40.8 [79]

Brad Keller RHP

Born: 07/27/95 Age: 25 Bats: R Throws: R
Height: 6'5" Weight: 250 Origin: Round 8, 2013 Draft (#240 overall)

YEAR	TEAM	LVL	AGE	W	L	SV	G	GS	IP	H	HR	BB/9	K/9	K	GB%	BABIP
2018	KC	MLB	22	9	6	0	41	20	140^1	133	7	3.2	6.2	96	54.5%	.294
2019	KC	MLB	23	7	14	0	28	28	165^1	154	15	3.8	6.6	122	50.4%	.283
2020	KC	MLB	24	5	3	0	9	9	54^2	39	2	2.8	5.8	35	51.6%	.233
2021 FS	KC	MLB	25	9	8	0	26	26	150	148	17	3.8	7.0	117	50.6%	.290
2021 DC	KC	MLB	25	9	8	0	25	25	147.7	145	17	3.8	7.0	115	50.6%	.290

Comparables: Lucas Giolito, Antonio Senzatela, Eduardo Rodriguez

Does Keller sell real estate on the side? He should consider it, if not, because the story of his season was location, location, location. Improved command of both his fastball and slider allowed him to live on the edges of the zone rather than the middle of it, leading to the best season of his career. Location! The slider has above-average downward break, and he was consistently able to keep it down and in the zone. Location! Down enough that if the hitter made contact, the result was generally a ground ball—nearly 53 percent of all balls in play for the right-hander were worm-burners. And ... results! There's not a lot of flash there—among the 81 pitchers who threw at least 50 innings he ranked 76th in strikeout rate—but you can't argue with the outcome.

YEAR	TEAM	LVL	AGE	WHIP	ERA	DRA-	WARP	MPH	FB%	WHF	CSP
2018	KC	MLB	22	1.30	3.08	108	0.6	96.2	69.8%	21.3%	
2019	KC	MLB	23	1.35	4.19	102	1.4	95.9	66.7%	19.9%	
2020	KC	MLB	24	1.02	2.47	91	0.7	94.8	59.2%	19.5%	
2021 FS	KC	MLB	25	1.41	4.34	101	1.4	95.7	65.5%	20.1%	46.7%
2021 DC	KC	MLB	25	1.41	4.34	101	1.3	95.7	65.5%	20.1%	46.7%

Brad Keller, continued

Pitch Shape vs LHH

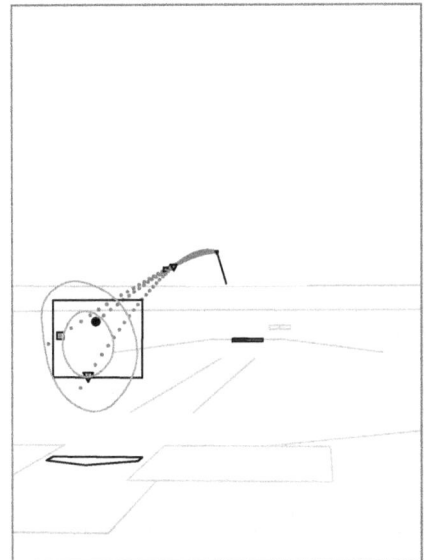

Pitch Shape vs RHH

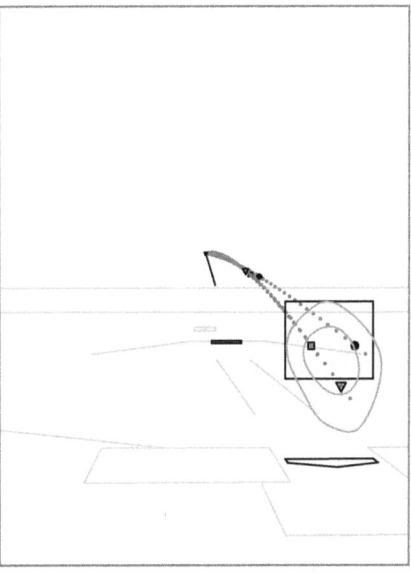

Type	Frequency	Velocity	H Movement	V Movement
● Fastball	38.2%	93.1 [102]	2.2 [143]	-16.4 [97]
□ Sinker	20.9%	92.7 [101]	-8.6 [133]	-20.4 [101]
▽ Slider	38.2%	84.8 [104]	5.4 [100]	-38.7 [86]

Kansas City Royals 2021

Ian Kennedy RHP
Born: 12/19/84   Age: 36   Bats: R   Throws: R
Height: 6'0"   Weight: 210   Origin: Round 1, 2006 Draft (#21 overall)

YEAR	TEAM	LVL	AGE	W	L	SV	G	GS	IP	H	HR	BB/9	K/9	K	GB%	BABIP
2018	KC	MLB	33	3	9	0	22	22	119²	125	20	3.0	7.9	105	29.6%	.302
2019	KC	MLB	34	3	2	30	63	0	63¹	64	6	2.4	10.4	73	43.4%	.349
2020	KC	MLB	35	0	2	0	15	1	14	20	7	3.2	9.6	15	37.5%	.325
2021 FS	KC	MLB	36	2	2	0	57	0	50	46	7	3.1	8.5	47	37.9%	.279
2021 DC	KC	MLB	36	3	3	0	63	0	55	51	8	3.1	8.5	52	37.9%	.279

Comparables: Aníbal Sánchez, Ervin Santana, Mike Fiers

On Royals radio broadcasts, longtime announcer Denny Mathews is known for his understated home run call: "Annnnnd ... gone!" he gruffly intones no matter if it's celebratory for a home team batsman or a call of despair for a local hurler. No Royals reliever was on the receiving end of such calls more than Kennedy, who, just a year after a revelatory move to the bullpen, lost velocity and a whole lotta baseballs over the fence. Playing out the final year of a five-year pact signed after the 2015 season, he hits the free agent market as a 36-year-old pitcher coming off the worst season of his career. Some club looking to add a reclamation project to their bullpen will take a flier.

YEAR	TEAM	LVL	AGE	WHIP	ERA	DRA-	WARP	MPH	FB%	WHF	CSP
2018	KC	MLB	33	1.38	4.66	118	0.0	93.7	58.6%	19.3%	
2019	KC	MLB	34	1.28	3.41	72	1.3	96.1	67.5%	24.3%	
2020	KC	MLB	35	1.79	9.00	131	-0.1	95.0	49.8%	21.5%	
2021 FS	KC	MLB	36	1.27	3.96	97	0.3	94.9	61.1%	21.8%	50.6%
2021 DC	KC	MLB	36	1.27	3.96	97	0.3	94.9	61.1%	21.8%	50.6%

Ian Kennedy, continued

Pitch Shape vs LHH

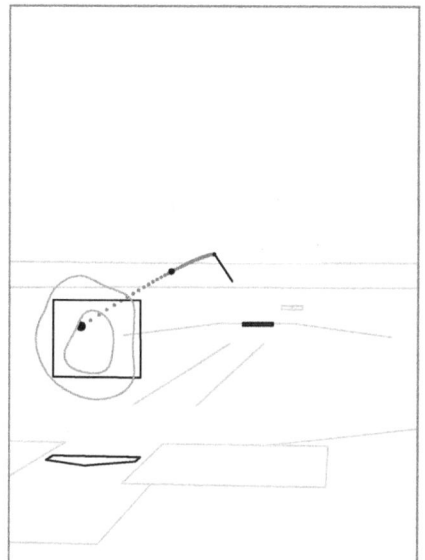

Pitch Shape vs RHH

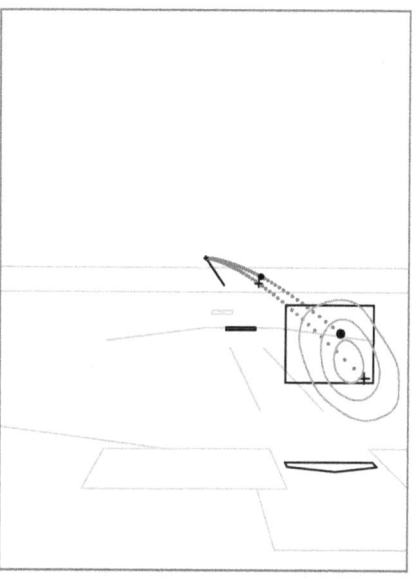

Type	Frequency	Velocity	H Movement	V Movement
● Fastball	49.1%	93.9 [104]	-9 [89]	-13.6 [105]
+ Cutter	31.7%	90 [111]	0 [88]	-21.7 [110]
▲ Changeup	7.2%	86.9 [107]	-11.2 [103]	-22.4 [114]
◇ Curveball	10.6%	80.7 [108]	8.1 [102]	-48.2 [100]

Mike Minor   LHP

Born: 12/26/87 Age: 33 Bats: R Throws: L
Height: 6'4" Weight: 210 Origin: Round 1, 2009 Draft (#7 overall)

YEAR	TEAM	LVL	AGE	W	L	SV	G	GS	IP	H	HR	BB/9	K/9	K	GB%	BABIP
2018	TEX	MLB	30	12	8	0	28	28	157	138	25	2.2	7.6	132	34.4%	.259
2019	TEX	MLB	31	14	10	0	32	32	208^1	190	30	2.9	8.6	200	40.5%	.288
2020	KC	MLB	32	1	6	0	12	11	56^2	50	11	3.2	9.8	62	35.3%	.269
2021 FS	KC	MLB	33	9	8	0	26	26	150	138	21	3.1	9.2	153	37.4%	.290
2021 DC	KC	MLB	33	9	8	0	27	27	140.3	129	20	3.1	9.2	143	37.4%	.290

Comparables: Trevor Cahill, Alex Cobb, Jhoulys Chacín

After calling for a pop-up to be dropped to notch his 200th strikeout in 2019, Minor learned baseball is 90 percent people imagining an unwritten rule, tricking themselves into believing that rule exists, and then getting mad about it. In 2020 he learned the other 10 percent is velocity, as his fastball lost another tick, for a total loss of 3.5 mph since 2017. This time the performance dipped with it and Minor struggled to prevent runs in both Texas, where he signed a three-year deal after the 2017 season, and Oakland, where he was traded mid-season. With below-average performance preventing him from getting deep into games, Minor probably wouldn't have hit 200 strikeouts across a full season, either, so maybe next time just catch the pop-up. He'll head to Kansas City on a two-year deal, where he rekindled his career once already.

YEAR	TEAM	LVL	AGE	WHIP	ERA	DRA-	WARP	MPH	FB%	WHF	CSP
2018	TEX	MLB	30	1.12	4.18	129	-0.9	94.9	49.5%	22.4%	
2019	TEX	MLB	31	1.24	3.59	82	3.9	94.3	44.7%	26.3%	
2020	KC	MLB	32	1.24	5.56	107	0.3	92.8	50.7%	27.3%	
2021 FS	KC	MLB	33	1.27	3.86	93	2.0	94.1	47.1%	25.7%	50.1%
2021 DC	KC	MLB	33	1.27	3.86	93	1.9	94.1	47.1%	25.7%	50.1%

Mike Minor, continued

Pitch Shape vs LHH

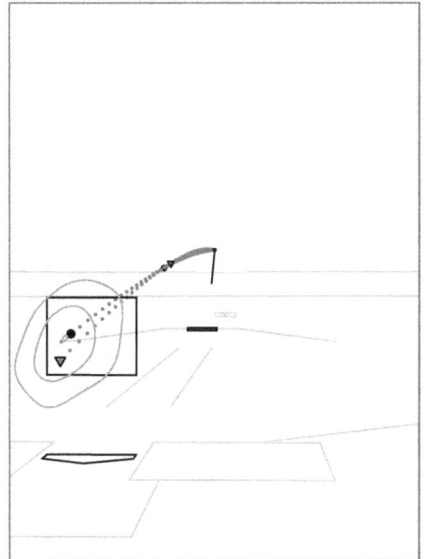

Pitch Shape vs RHH

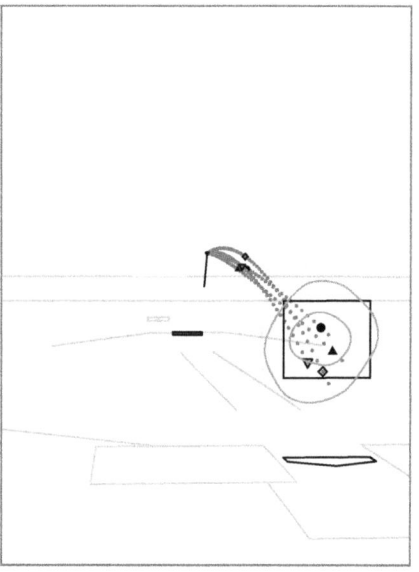

Type	Frequency	Velocity	H Movement	V Movement
● Fastball	50.6%	90.8 [94]	1 [127]	-17.2 [94]
▲ Changeup	22.1%	85.6 [102]	15 [83]	-23.4 [111]
▽ Slider	20.7%	85.8 [108]	-5.3 [100]	-31.5 [107]
◇ Curveball	6.4%	80.4 [107]	-6.9 [97]	-49.3 [98]

Kansas City Royals 2021

Jake Newberry   RHP

Born: 11/20/94   Age: 26   Bats: R   Throws: R
Height: 6'2"   Weight: 205   Origin: Round 37, 2012 Draft (#1123 overall)

YEAR	TEAM	LVL	AGE	W	L	SV	G	GS	IP	H	HR	BB/9	K/9	K	GB%	BABIP
2018	NWA	AA	23	2	0	12	25	0	29²	29	2	2.4	11.2	37	32.5%	.360
2018	OMA	AAA	23	3	0	3	16	0	20	13	1	2.7	7.2	16	49.1%	.231
2018	KC	MLB	23	2	0	0	14	0	13¹	13	3	6.1	7.4	11	32.5%	.270
2019	OMA	AAA	24	2	2	0	22	0	28	29	3	4.5	9.6	30	37.0%	.342
2019	KC	MLB	24	1	0	0	27	0	31	29	7	4.6	8.4	29	34.1%	.262
2020	KC	MLB	25	1	0	1	20	0	22	20	3	4.9	9.8	24	37.5%	.321
2021 FS	KC	MLB	26	2	3	0	57	0	50	46	8	4.4	9.2	50	36.1%	.286
2021 DC	KC	MLB	26	2	3	0	57	0	61	56	9	4.4	9.2	62	36.1%	.286

Comparables: Michael Tonkin, Trevor Gott, Evan Phillips

As rosters and bullpens expand, there will always be room for guys like Newberry. Of his 20 appearances in 2020, only two came while the Royals held a lead. But aside from a couple of poor outings, he did his job and kept his team within shouting distance. For the first time in his major-league career, he featured the slider more than his fastball. Smart move. The slider features more drop than break and comes with plenty of swing and miss—opponents whiffed on 48 percent of their swings against the pitch. When contact is made on the slider, it's generally weak. He's not going to be called on to secure the lead in the seventh or to bridge to the closer in the eighth. He's not a fireman, nor one who will rack up the saves. But he's a steady presence in the back of a bullpen. That's worth something.

YEAR	TEAM	LVL	AGE	WHIP	ERA	DRA-	WARP	MPH	FB%	WHF	CSP
2018	NWA	AA	23	1.25	2.12	56	0.7				
2018	OMA	AAA	23	0.95	0.90	69	0.4				
2018	KC	MLB	23	1.65	4.72	125	-0.1	95.3	54.8%	26.5%	
2019	OMA	AAA	24	1.54	3.86	79	0.6				
2019	KC	MLB	24	1.45	3.77	152	-0.7	95.5	52.5%	27.5%	
2020	KC	MLB	25	1.45	4.09	114	0.0	95.0	45.2%	36.2%	
2021 FS	KC	MLB	26	1.42	4.61	106	0.1	95.2	49.3%	31.5%	42.8%
2021 DC	KC	MLB	26	1.42	4.61	106	0.1	95.2	49.3%	31.5%	42.8%

Jake Newberry, continued

Pitch Shape vs LHH

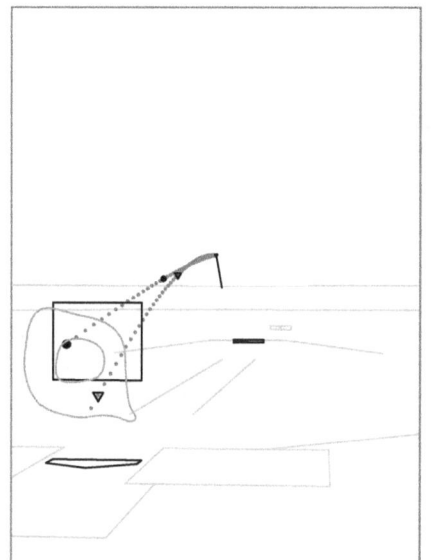

Pitch Shape vs RHH

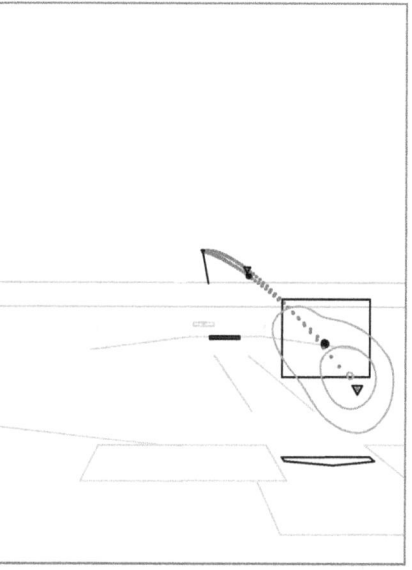

Type	Frequency	Velocity	H Movement	V Movement
● Fastball	45.2%	93.6 [103]	-2.3 [121]	-13.6 [105]
▲ Changeup	3.6%	87 [107]	-7 [125]	-21.7 [116]
▽ Slider	51.2%	83.5 [98]	4.4 [97]	-36.1 [93]

Brady Singer RHP

Born: 08/04/96 Age: 24 Bats: R Throws: R
Height: 6'5" Weight: 210 Origin: Round 1, 2018 Draft (#18 overall)

YEAR	TEAM	LVL	AGE	W	L	SV	G	GS	IP	H	HR	BB/9	K/9	K	GB%	BABIP
2019	WIL	HI-A	22	5	2	0	10	10	57^2	51	1	2.0	8.3	53	54.8%	.327
2019	NWA	AA	22	7	3	0	16	16	90^2	86	8	2.6	8.4	85	49.3%	.304
2020	KC	MLB	23	4	5	0	12	12	64^1	52	8	3.2	8.5	61	53.7%	.260
2021 FS	KC	MLB	24	9	8	0	26	26	150	142	17	3.8	8.3	137	50.1%	.294
2021 DC	KC	MLB	24	9	8	0	25	25	139.7	133	16	3.8	8.3	128	50.1%	.294

Comparables: Jered Weaver, T.J. Zeuch, Michael Fulmer

Singer was the first of five college arms drafted in the first two rounds of the 2018 draft by the Royals, and he continued to lead the way in 2020. He was the first of his class to reach the majors, where he ultimately led all rookies in innings pitched and strikeouts. Singer relies on a sinker/slider combo that induced the fourth-highest ground ball rate among qualified starters. The focus heading into this year was the third pitch in his arsenal—a newly refined change. After throwing it only five percent of the time, he's still figuring out how to trust the pitch as it continues to be a work in progress. The Royals were happy with how he was able to command the *cambio* though, and it will again be the focus of his offseason. He may not bring the highest upside of the Royals' young guns, but he's at the head of the class.

YEAR	TEAM	LVL	AGE	WHIP	ERA	DRA-	WARP	MPH	FB%	WHF	CSP
2019	WIL	HI-A	22	1.11	1.87	105	-0.1				
2019	NWA	AA	22	1.24	3.47	81	1.1				
2020	KC	MLB	23	1.17	4.06	87	1.0	95.2	57.9%	24.3%	
2021 FS	KC	MLB	24	1.37	4.22	98	1.6	95.2	57.9%	24.3%	47.8%
2021 DC	KC	MLB	24	1.37	4.22	98	1.5	95.2	57.9%	24.3%	47.8%

Brady Singer, continued

Pitch Shape vs LHH

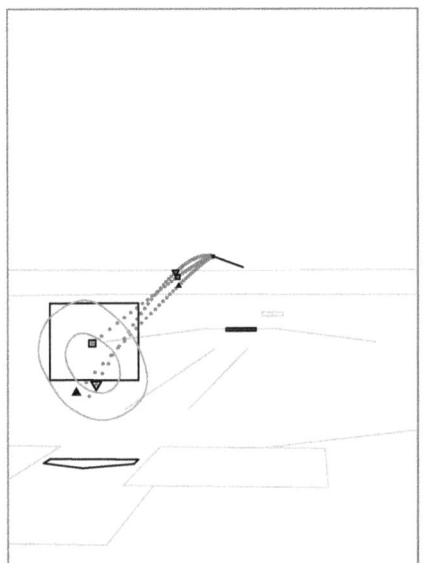

Pitch Shape vs RHH

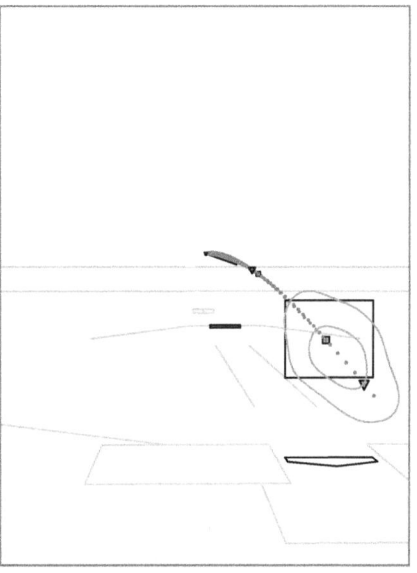

Type	Frequency	Velocity	H Movement	V Movement
☐ Sinker	57.4%	93.5 [106]	-12.2 [106]	-17.2 [111]
▲ Changeup	4.7%	88 [111]	-14 [88]	-22.2 [114]
▽ Slider	37.4%	83.3 [97]	4.2 [96]	-36.6 [92]

Josh Staumont RHP

Born: 12/21/93 Age: 27 Bats: R Throws: R
Height: 6'3" Weight: 205 Origin: Round 2, 2015 Draft (#64 overall)

YEAR	TEAM	LVL	AGE	W	L	SV	G	GS	IP	H	HR	BB/9	K/9	K	GB%	BABIP
2018	OMA	AAA	24	2	5	1	41	5	74^1	59	4	6.3	12.5	103	41.3%	.331
2019	OMA	AAA	25	1	5	2	32	12	51^1	31	4	6.5	13.0	74	48.6%	.262
2019	KC	MLB	25	0	0	0	16	0	19^1	21	4	4.7	7.0	15	32.3%	.293
2020	KC	MLB	26	2	1	0	26	0	25^2	20	2	5.6	13.0	37	28.6%	.333
2021 FS	KC	MLB	27	2	3	8	57	0	50	43	7	6.8	12.0	66	36.3%	.307
2021 DC	KC	MLB	27	2	3	8	57	0	61	53	9	6.8	12.0	81	36.3%	.307

Comparables: Lucas Sims, Drew Anderson, Robert Stephenson

Heater. Smoke. Gas. Cheddar. Pick your slang. Staumont threw 28 pitches over 100 mph last year, third-most in the majors. He maxed out at a blistering 102.2 mph. Then there's the hook. Yakker. Hammer. Uncle Charlie. Now go ahead and pick your curveball slang. He also features a knee-buckling 12-to-6 breaking ball that comes in 20 mph slower than the fastball. We know that hitting is incredibly difficult ... against a pitcher like this, how is any kind of contact ever possible? A repertoire this lethal gets you some Twitter time from @PitchingNinja, with good reason. If there's a knock here, it's that the control isn't always there. That will probably keep him from closing out wins, but when he brings a flamethrower and an axis-altering hook to the mound, who really cares what inning he pitches? If you buy a ticket, this is the guy you want to see. When he's on, it's tons of fun. If manager Mike Matheny is summoning him from the bullpen, we're calling the neighbors and waking the kids.

YEAR	TEAM	LVL	AGE	WHIP	ERA	DRA-	WARP	MPH	FB%	WHF	CSP
2018	OMA	AAA	24	1.49	3.51	76	1.4				
2019	OMA	AAA	25	1.32	3.16	43	2.1				
2019	KC	MLB	25	1.60	3.72	163	-0.5	98.2	69.6%	22.7%	
2020	KC	MLB	26	1.40	2.45	91	0.4	101.2	72.5%	36.7%	
2021 FS	KC	MLB	27	1.63	5.39	115	-0.2	100.3	71.6%	32.3%	46.1%
2021 DC	KC	MLB	27	1.63	5.39	115	-0.2	100.3	71.6%	32.3%	46.1%

Josh Staumont, continued

Pitch Shape vs LHH

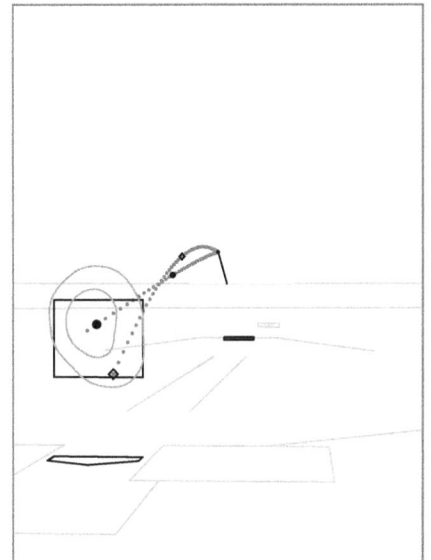

Pitch Shape vs RHH

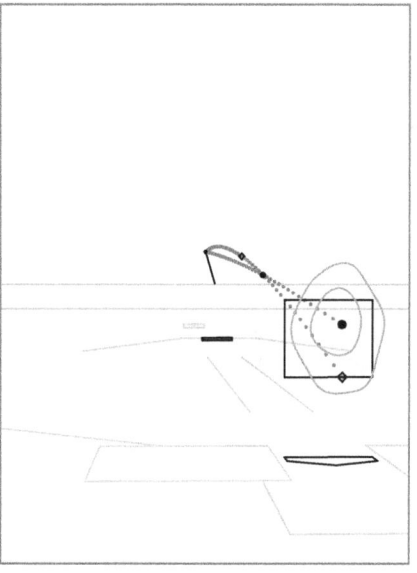

Type	Frequency	Velocity	H Movement	V Movement
● Fastball	68.6%	98.2 [118]	-3.7 [114]	-9 [118]
☐ Sinker	3.8%	99.2 [135]	-9.9 [123]	-10.6 [132]
◇ Curveball	27.5%	82.4 [115]	8.3 [103]	-50.2 [96]

Kyle Zimmer RHP

Born: 09/13/91 Age: 29 Bats: R Throws: R
Height: 6'3" Weight: 225 Origin: Round 1, 2012 Draft (#5 overall)

YEAR	TEAM	LVL	AGE	W	L	SV	G	GS	IP	H	HR	BB/9	K/9	K	GB%	BABIP
2019	OMA	AAA	27	2	4	1	37	12	54	46	6	5.5	8.7	52	44.4%	.276
2019	KC	MLB	27	0	1	0	15	0	18^1	28	2	9.3	8.8	18	41.5%	.413
2020	KC	MLB	28	1	0	0	16	1	23	14	0	3.9	10.2	26	51.9%	.259
2021 FS	KC	MLB	29	2	2	0	57	0	50	44	5	5.2	9.5	52	42.8%	.289
2021 DC	KC	MLB	29	2	2	0	51	0	55	48	6	5.2	9.5	57	42.8%	.289

Comparables: Brooks Pounders, Juan Minaya, Luke Farrell

Zimmer's long and winding road saw myriad injuries and setbacks, *r*ecoveries and *r*ehabs, culminating in *r*ediscovered velocity, a 2019 major-league debut, and a lack of command. *R*ebuilt mechanics courtesy of an encounter with Tom House led to *r*esounding success last year. It should be noted the Royals handled him with care, pitching him on *r*epeat days only once, although they did let him go multiple innings in six of his outings. While a starter's profile still lurks, the Royals remain committed to him as a *r*eliever.

YEAR	TEAM	LVL	AGE	WHIP	ERA	DRA-	WARP	MPH	FB%	WHF	CSP
2019	OMA	AAA	27	1.46	4.33	72	1.5				
2019	KC	MLB	27	2.56	10.80	174	-0.6	98.1	60.9%	26.6%	
2020	KC	MLB	28	1.04	1.57	77	0.5	95.6	48.1%	30.0%	
2021 FS	KC	MLB	29	1.46	4.35	99	0.3	96.7	53.7%	28.5%	46.5%
2021 DC	KC	MLB	29	1.46	4.35	99	0.3	96.7	53.7%	28.5%	46.5%

Kyle Zimmer, continued

Pitch Shape vs LHH

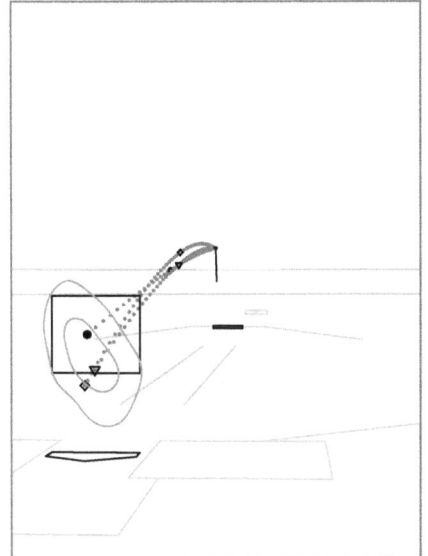

Pitch Shape vs RHH

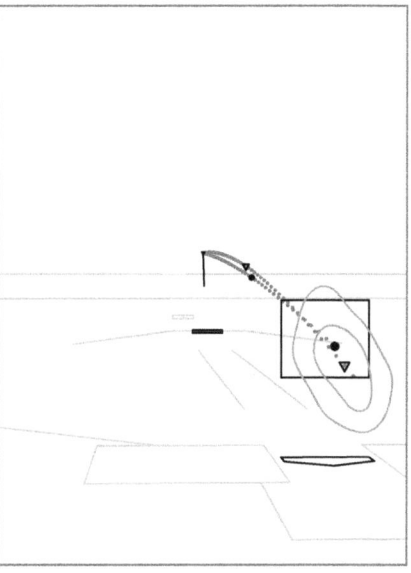

Type	Frequency	Velocity	H Movement	V Movement
● Fastball	48.1%	94.3 [105]	-0.3 [130]	-14 [103]
▲ Changeup	3.5%	86.4 [105]	-5.6 [132]	-23.4 [111]
▽ Slider	34.6%	83.1 [96]	2 [88]	-33.7 [100]
◇ Curveball	13.8%	77.5 [96]	3.1 [82]	-52.1 [92]

Kansas City Royals 2021

Tyler Zuber RHP

Born: 06/16/95 Age: 26 Bats: R Throws: R
Height: 5'11" Weight: 175 Origin: Round 6, 2017 Draft (#180 overall)

YEAR	TEAM	LVL	AGE	W	L	SV	G	GS	IP	H	HR	BB/9	K/9	K	GB%	BABIP
2018	LEX	LO-A	23	2	2	9	23	0	29	26	4	1.2	14.9	48	31.1%	.386
2018	WIL	HI-A	23	1	4	9	20	0	22	22	1	3.7	9.0	22	41.5%	.333
2019	WIL	HI-A	24	3	2	11	21	0	29^1	16	0	3.4	11.7	38	34.4%	.254
2019	NWA	AA	24	1	2	10	22	0	26	18	2	1.7	10.4	30	27.0%	.276
2020	KC	MLB	25	1	2	0	23	0	22	15	4	8.2	12.3	30	37.5%	.256
2021 FS	KC	MLB	26	2	2	0	57	0	50	44	7	4.4	10.6	58	37.0%	.298
2021 DC	KC	MLB	26	2	2	0	57	0	61	54	8	4.4	10.6	72	37.0%	.298

Comparables: Tony Gonsolin, Zac Reininger, Jacob Webb

Of the 22 innings Zuber pitched, he retired the side in order only five times, issuing 20 free passes over those frames. Zuber should leave the highwire acts to the Flying Wallendas if he wants to stick around.

YEAR	TEAM	LVL	AGE	WHIP	ERA	DRA-	WARP	MPH	FB%	WHF	CSP
2018	LEX	LO-A	23	1.03	3.10	48	0.9				
2018	WIL	HI-A	23	1.41	4.91	80	0.3				
2019	WIL	HI-A	24	0.92	1.23	55	0.7				
2019	NWA	AA	24	0.88	2.42	60	0.5				
2020	KC	MLB	25	1.59	4.09	102	0.2	96.1	44.4%	25.6%	
2021 FS	KC	MLB	26	1.38	4.31	99	0.3	96.1	44.4%	25.6%	44.8%
2021 DC	KC	MLB	26	1.38	4.31	99	0.3	96.1	44.4%	25.6%	44.8%

Tyler Zuber, continued

Pitch Shape vs LHH

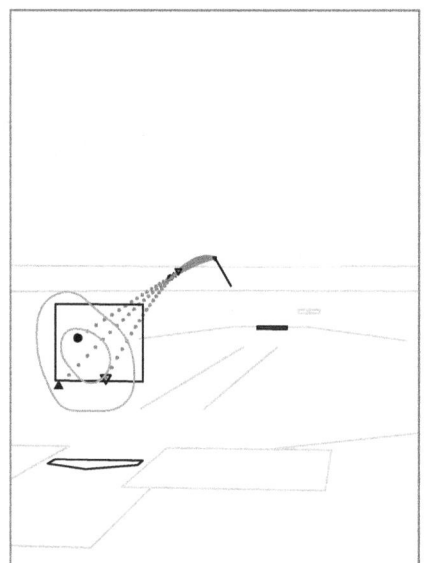

Pitch Shape vs RHH

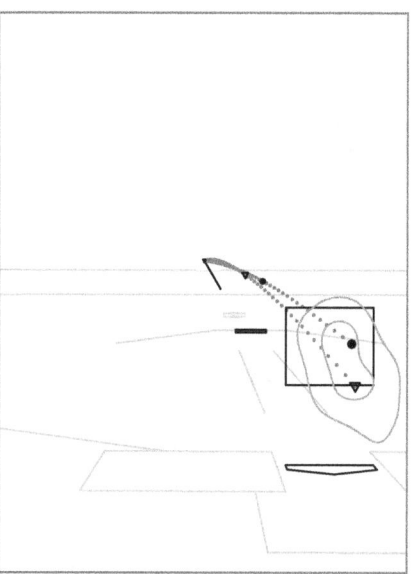

Type	Frequency	Velocity	H Movement	V Movement
● Fastball	43.7%	94.3 [105]	-7.2 [98]	-14.2 [103]
▲ Changeup	9.8%	86.3 [104]	-10.2 [108]	-34.2 [82]
▽ Slider	34.6%	84.2 [101]	7.1 [107]	-35.7 [94]
◇ Curveball	10.3%	81.2 [110]	10.4 [111]	-45.4 [107]

Kansas City Royals 2021

PLAYER COMMENTS WITHOUT GRAPHS

Andrew Benintendi LF
Born: 07/06/94   Age: 27   Bats: L   Throws: L
Height: 5'9"   Weight: 180   Origin: Round 1, 2015 Draft (#7 overall)

YEAR	TEAM	LVL	AGE	PA	R	2B	3B	HR	RBI	BB	K	SB	CS	AVG/OBP/SLG
2018	BOS	MLB	23	661	103	41	6	16	87	71	106	21	3	.290/.366/.465
2019	BOS	MLB	24	615	72	40	5	13	68	59	140	10	3	.266/.343/.431
2020	BOS	MLB	25	52	4	1	0	0	1	11	17	1	2	.103/.314/.128
2021 FS	KC	MLB	26	600	78	27	4	15	55	69	131	13	4	.240/.335/.395
2021 DC	KC	MLB	26	587	76	26	4	14	54	67	129	13	4	.240/.335/.395

Comparables: Dusty Rhodes, Christian Yelich, Nolan Reimold

As Benintendi goes, so go the Red Sox. At his peak, Benny with the Good Hair served as a linchpin of the best team in franchise history. More often, he's underperformed relative to his talent. And in 2020, he may as well not have existed. Benintendi was limited to a handful of games thanks to a rib injury, and with the Sox actively tanking there was no impetus for him to return to action. When he did play he was terrible, and while the sample size is quite small it was concerning to see Benintendi look so lost at the plate following his disappointing 2019. He won't turn 27 until halfway through this season, but we're now two-plus years removed from Benintendi looking like anything special. It's strange to think that a sweet-swinging lefty could need a change of scenery *away* from Boston, but it's sure starting to feel that way.

YEAR	TEAM	LVL	AGE	PA	DRC+	BABIP	BRR	FRAA	WARP
2018	BOS	MLB	23	661	117	.328	-1.1	LF(129): 8.2, CF(24): -2.6	3.7
2019	BOS	MLB	24	615	94	.333	0.8	LF(131): -5.7, CF(12): 1.5	0.9
2020	BOS	MLB	25	52	80	.182	0.2	LF(13): 0.2	0.0
2021 FS	KC	MLB	26	600	101	.294	0.8	LF 0, CF -2	1.6
2021 DC	KC	MLB	26	587	101	.294	0.8	LF 0, CF -2	1.5

Lucius Fox   SS

Born: 07/02/97   Age: 24   Bats: S   Throws: R
Height: 6'1"   Weight: 185   Origin: International Free Agent, 2015

YEAR	TEAM	LVL	AGE	PA	R	2B	3B	HR	RBI	BB	K	SB	CS	AVG/OBP/SLG
2018	CHA	HI-A	20	404	54	17	1	2	30	42	79	23	7	.282/.371/.353
2018	MTG	AA	20	120	14	3	1	1	9	8	20	6	2	.221/.284/.298
2019	MTG	AA	21	431	60	16	8	3	33	53	89	37	11	.230/.340/.342
2019	DUR	AAA	21	49	6	0	1	0	1	6	15	2	0	.143/.250/.190
2021 FS	KC	MLB	23	600	59	23	4	7	47	51	176	20	8	.214/.293/.314
2021 DC	KC	MLB	23	65	6	2	0	0	5	5	19	2	1	.214/.293/.314

Comparables: Tyler Wade, Hanley Ramirez, Eugenio Suárez

If the Royals had a profile on Tinder, they would swipe right on speedy athletes who struggle to get on base consistently and lack a power projection. They matched with Fox in a midseason trade with Tampa in exchange for Brett Phillips.

YEAR	TEAM	LVL	AGE	PA	DRC+	BABIP	BRR	FRAA	WARP
2018	CHA	HI-A	20	404	124	.358	2.1	SS(79): -1.5	1.8
2018	MTG	AA	20	120	70	.259	0.6	SS(26): -0.7	-0.1
2019	MTG	AA	21	431	106	.293	0.6	SS(79): -3.9, 2B(12): 1.4, 3B(9): 1.4	2.0
2019	DUR	AAA	21	49	47	.222	0.6	SS(12): 0.4, 2B(1): -0.1	0.0
2021 FS	KC	MLB	23	600	69	.304	2.0	SS -1, 2B 0	-0.6
2021 DC	KC	MLB	23	65	69	.304	0.2	SS 0	-0.1

Cam Gallagher   C

Born: 12/06/92   Age: 28   Bats: R   Throws: R
Height: 6'3"   Weight: 230   Origin: Round 2, 2011 Draft (#65 overall)

YEAR	TEAM	LVL	AGE	PA	R	2B	3B	HR	RBI	BB	K	SB	CS	AVG/OBP/SLG
2018	OMA	AAA	25	303	28	13	0	4	42	26	38	1	0	.265/.334/.358
2018	KC	MLB	25	69	5	3	0	1	7	3	15	0	0	.206/.250/.302
2019	KC	MLB	26	142	14	7	0	3	12	11	28	0	1	.238/.312/.365
2020	KC	MLB	27	60	10	5	0	1	3	6	11	0	0	.283/.356/.434
2021 FS	KC	MLB	28	600	65	25	1	12	59	49	121	0	1	.238/.308/.363
2021 DC	KC	MLB	28	120	13	5	0	2	11	9	24	0	0	.238/.308/.363

Comparables: Bruce Bochy, Sal Fasano, Larry Howard

Kansas City Royals 2021

Being a backup catcher on the Royals when Salvador Perez is healthy is a bit like being a weatherman in San Diego: Nobody cares. But when an eye ailment sent the first-stringer to the sidelines, the understudy was ready. Gallagher enjoyed the finest offensive season of his oft-interrupted major-league career, posting career highs in rate stats across the board. As a reward, he is preparing his lines for 2021, just in case he's called upon again.

YEAR	TEAM	P. COUNT	FRM RUNS	BLK RUNS	THRW RUNS	TOT RUNS
2018	KC	2414	1.5	1.0	0.0	2.6
2018	OMA	9980	11.3	0.3	0.1	11.7
2019	KC	5506	3.7	0.9	-0.3	4.3
2020	KC	2736	-0.1	-0.1	0.0	-0.1
2021	KC	4810	1.3	0.8	-0.1	2.0
2021	KC	4810	1.3	-0.4	-0.1	0.9

YEAR	TEAM	LVL	AGE	PA	DRC+	BABIP	BRR	FRAA	WARP
2018	OMA	AAA	25	303	84	.294	-2.0	C(72): 11.9	1.5
2018	KC	MLB	25	69	84	.250	-1.6	C(20): 2.4	0.3
2019	KC	MLB	26	142	91	.281	-0.6	C(44): 3.8	0.9
2020	KC	MLB	27	60	91	.341	1.0	C(25): -0.4	0.2
2021 FS	KC	MLB	28	600	87	.284	-0.8	C 7	2.2
2021 DC	KC	MLB	28	120	87	.284	-0.2	C 2	0.5

Kyle Isbel OF
Born: 03/03/97   Age: 24   Bats: L   Throws: R
Height: 5'11"   Weight: 183   Origin: Round 3, 2018 Draft (#94 overall)

YEAR	TEAM	LVL	AGE	PA	R	2B	3B	HR	RBI	BB	K	SB	CS	AVG/OBP/SLG
2018	IDF	ROK	21	119	27	10	1	4	18	14	17	12	3	.381/.454/.610
2018	LEX	LO-A	21	174	30	12	1	3	14	12	43	12	3	.289/.345/.434
2019	ROY	ROK	22	27	9	2	0	2	7	2	5	3	1	.360/.407/.680
2019	WIL	HI-A	22	214	26	7	3	5	23	15	44	8	3	.216/.282/.361
2021 FS	KC	MLB	24	600	52	23	3	12	57	40	173	15	7	.214/.272/.336

Comparables: Paulo Orlando, Abraham Almonte, Rosell Herrera

There aren't a lot of hitting prospects in the Royals' system, especially compared to the young arms that are on the edge of a breakthrough. With good pitch recognition and decent enough bat speed, Isbel represents one of the batters with the most potential. He was scorching hot to open 2019 until a hamate injury sidelined him for a couple of months and ultimately sabotaged his second half. He got back on track in the AFL and then COVID-19 meant he lost an entire minor-league season—although he did spend August and September at the club's alternate training site. Like just about every other prospect toiling in the mid-minors, he'll do well to get back on the field with a full season of competition. And if this baseball thing doesn't work out, he could always hit the lanes. It's likely he's the second-best bowler in baseball next to Mookie Betts, but that's an argument for the 2021 edition of Bowling Prospectus.

YEAR	TEAM	LVL	AGE	PA	DRC+	BABIP	BRR	FRAA	WARP
2018	IDF	ROK	21	119		.429			
2018	LEX	LO-A	21	174	110	.377	2.8	CF(27): 0.8, LF(11): -0.5	0.7
2019	ROY	ROK	22	27		.389			
2019	WIL	HI-A	22	214	85	.253	1.8	CF(32): -2.3, RF(12): 0.5	0.2
2021 FS	KC	MLB	24	600	66	.287	1.5	CF 3, RF 2	-0.2

Erick Pena CF
Born: 02/20/03   Age: 18   Bats: L   Throws: R
Height: 6'3"   Weight: 180   Origin: International Free Agent, 2019

Do you dig tools? Peña may just be the prospect for you. The Royals splashed the cash in the 2019 IFA period, awarding the center fielder with a $3.8 million bonus and it didn't take long for the Carlos Beltran comps to surface. The youngster already has balance and bat speed in the toolkit with plenty of room to grow. The Royals had enough faith to keep him in Kansas City after the regular season ended so he could take part in instructional league games where the competition level was somewhere between Double and Triple-A. The reports were glowing. The Yankees' Jasson Dominguez will be the name dominating headlines from this J2 class for a good while yet, but don't sleep on Peña's significant upside.

Bubba Starling CF
Born: 08/03/92   Age: 28   Bats: R   Throws: R
Height: 6'4"   Weight: 215   Origin: Round 1, 2011 Draft (#5 overall)

YEAR	TEAM	LVL	AGE	PA	R	2B	3B	HR	RBI	BB	K	SB	CS	AVG/OBP/SLG
2018	OMA	AAA	25	41	5	2	0	0	2	5	6	1	0	.257/.350/.314
2019	OMA	AAA	26	285	34	11	2	7	38	21	59	9	3	.310/.358/.448
2019	KC	MLB	26	197	26	7	0	4	12	9	56	2	0	.215/.255/.317
2020	KC	MLB	27	64	5	1	0	1	5	4	27	0	0	.169/.219/.237
2021 FS	KC	MLB	28	600	49	18	2	13	55	39	215	3	2	.187/.246/.303

Comparables: Stevie Wilkerson, Hiram Bocachica, Billy Beane

The former fifth-overall pick from suburban Kansas City just wrapped his 10th year in the organization. The pitch recognition issues that plagued Starling in his early years haven't been resolved and his defense in center— once a calling card due to his athleticism and speed—has been spotty at best. Sadly, the local kid didn't make good.

Kansas City Royals 2021

YEAR	TEAM	LVL	AGE	PA	DRC+	BABIP	BRR	FRAA	WARP
2018	OMA	AAA	25	41	87	.310	-0.2	CF(10): -0.7, RF(1): -0.1	-0.1
2019	OMA	AAA	26	285	100	.374	0.0	CF(51): 3.1, RF(18): 2.2	1.4
2019	KC	MLB	26	197	63	.286	3.8	CF(36): 5.8, RF(23): -0.4, LF(6): -0.6	0.5
2020	KC	MLB	27	64	49	.281	0.4	CF(29): -2.5, LF(1): -0.0, RF(1): -0.0	-0.5
2021 FS	KC	MLB	28	600	51	.274	-0.1	CF 4, RF 1	-1.6

Meibrys Viloria C
Born: 02/15/97   Age: 24   Bats: L   Throws: R
Height: 5'11"   Weight: 225   Origin: International Free Agent, 2013

YEAR	TEAM	LVL	AGE	PA	R	2B	3B	HR	RBI	BB	K	SB	CS	AVG/OBP/SLG
2018	WIL	HI-A	21	407	34	16	1	6	44	40	75	2	1	.260/.342/.360
2018	KC	MLB	21	29	4	2	0	0	4	1	9	0	0	.259/.286/.333
2019	NWA	AA	22	248	21	12	0	1	24	24	60	2	0	.264/.344/.332
2019	KC	MLB	22	148	7	7	0	1	15	10	44	0	1	.211/.259/.286
2020	KC	MLB	23	24	1	1	0	0	0	2	9	0	0	.190/.292/.238
2021 FS	KC	MLB	24	600	57	21	1	9	50	45	172	0	1	.207/.275/.306
2021 DC	KC	MLB	24	30	2	1	0	0	2	2	8	0	0	.207/.275/.306

Comparables: Dave Duncan, Ben Davis, Ron Karkovice

The pandemic meant that for the second consecutive year, Viloria missed out on what should have been competitive developmental time in the minor leagues. Although he spent most of his summer at the Royals' alternate site, he did manage a call-up when Salvador Perez landed on the IL with blurred vision. The tools remain the same—raw. He has a strong arm behind the dish but could improve his framing. On the flip side he hasn't shown much in his cups of coffee, but what should we expect from a 23-year-old who has a half-season of Double-A ball under his belt. Out of options heading into 2021, the Royals will have to get creative—and lucky—if they are to get him the additional developmental time he so desperately needs.

YEAR	TEAM	P. COUNT	FRM RUNS	BLK RUNS	THRW RUNS	TOT RUNS
2018	KC	1178	0.0	-0.8	0.0	-0.9
2019	KC	5921	-4.0	0.0	0.3	-3.7
2019	NWA	8588	-7.7	0.0	0.3	-7.5
2020	KC	1408	-0.6	-0.2	0.0	-0.8
2021	KC	1202	-0.5	-0.2	0.0	-0.7
2021	KC	1202	-0.5	-0.3	0.0	-0.8

YEAR	TEAM	LVL	AGE	PA	DRC+	BABIP	BRR	FRAA	WARP
2018	WIL	HI-A	21	407	107	.313	-2.8	C(88): 2.8	1.3
2018	KC	MLB	21	29	73	.389	0.1	C(10): -1.0	0.0
2019	NWA	AA	22	248	97	.358	0.9	C(58): -6.3	0.5
2019	KC	MLB	22	148	59	.293	-0.5	C(41): -3.6	-0.4
2020	KC	MLB	23	24	68	.333	-0.2	C(15): 0.4	-0.1
2021 FS	KC	MLB	24	600	60	.283	-0.7	C -10	-1.7
2021 DC	KC	MLB	24	30	60	.283	0.0	C -1	-0.1

Bobby Witt Jr. SS

Born: 06/14/00   Age: 21   Bats: R   Throws: R
Height: 6'1"   Weight: 190   Origin: Round 1, 2019 Draft (#2 overall)

YEAR	TEAM	LVL	AGE	PA	R	2B	3B	HR	RBI	BB	K	SB	CS	AVG/OBP/SLG
2019	ROY	ROK	19	180	30	2	5	1	27	13	35	9	1	.262/.317/.354
2021 FS	KC	MLB	21	600	43	18	4	7	48	30	193	12	3	.197/.241/.287

Comparables: Erick Mejia, Erik González, Michael A. Taylor

There's a certain amount of hype that accompanies the second-overall selection in the draft. The hype accelerated for Witt following a successful—if shortened—spring training, a robust summer camp and a productive turn in the Royals' alternate site in August and September. At just 20 years old and a year and a half removed from high school, dammit if the kid didn't carry himself like a pro. Sure, he's been around the game his entire life, thanks to his dad who enjoyed a 16-year major league career, but still, this was something else. At the plate, you could see the quick hands, the bat speed, the feel for the barrel. In the field you could see the range, the glove action and the strong arm. And to round it off, you could see the plus-plus athleticism. We're talking about a potential five-tool talent. And as they say in Dollar Sign On The Muscle, the kid has the good face.

YEAR	TEAM	LVL	AGE	PA	DRC+	BABIP	BRR	FRAA	WARP
2019	ROY	ROK	19	180		.323			
2021 FS	KC	MLB	21	600	44	.284	1.3	SS 5	-1.8

Ronald Bolaños RHP

Born: 08/23/96   Age: 24   Bats: R   Throws: R
Height: 6'2"   Weight: 230   Origin: International Free Agent, 2016

YEAR	TEAM	LVL	AGE	W	L	SV	G	GS	IP	H	HR	BB/9	K/9	K	GB%	BABIP
2018	LE	HI-A	21	6	9	0	25	23	125	138	13	3.6	8.5	118	42.6%	.342
2019	LE	HI-A	22	5	2	0	10	10	53^2	37	4	3.9	9.1	54	48.2%	.246
2019	AMA	AA	22	8	5	0	15	13	76^2	71	7	3.5	10.3	88	46.5%	.335
2019	SD	MLB	22	0	2	0	5	3	19^2	17	3	5.5	8.7	19	39.3%	.264
2020	KC	MLB	23	0	2	0	2	2	3^2	8	2	7.4	4.9	2	53.3%	.462
2021 FS	*KC*	*MLB*	*24*	*2*	*3*	*0*	*57*	*0*	*50*	*49*	*7*	*5.1*	*8.2*	*45*	*43.9%*	*.296*
2021 DC	*KC*	*MLB*	*24*	*4*	*3*	*0*	*29*	*6*	*50.3*	*49*	*7*	*5.1*	*8.2*	*45*	*43.9%*	*.296*

Comparables: Chris Flexen, Touki Toussaint, Blake Snell

A dearth of starters to open the season pressed Bolaños—acquired in a summer camp deal from San Diego for reliever Tim Hill—into the rotation, but the prospect struggled to keep runners off the bases in a pair of abbreviated starts. The Cuban, a member of the Padres' heralded J2 class of 2016, possesses an electric arm but is still searching for command. Even in his short stint in the bigs, it was obvious he was catching far too much of the plate, especially with the heater coming in around 95 mph. Unfortunately, the slider was living a bit too down the middle, as well. Exiled to the alternate site after the second week of the season, he'll remain in the Royals' plans in some shape going forward. But electricity isn't much use if you can't harness the current.

YEAR	TEAM	LVL	AGE	WHIP	ERA	DRA-	WARP	MPH	FB%	WHF	CSP
2018	LE	HI-A	21	1.50	5.11	97	0.7				
2019	LE	HI-A	22	1.12	2.85	69	1.1				
2019	AMA	AA	22	1.32	4.23	100	0.0				
2019	SD	MLB	22	1.47	5.95	123	-0.1	97.8	62.7%	24.1%	
2020	KC	MLB	23	3.00	12.27	109	0.0	98.3	58.9%	15.6%	
2021 FS	*KC*	*MLB*	*24*	*1.55*	*5.26*	*117*	*-0.2*	*97.9*	*61.8%*	*22.1%*	*46.3%*
2021 DC	*KC*	*MLB*	*24*	*1.55*	*5.26*	*117*	*0.0*	*97.9*	*61.8%*	*22.1%*	*46.3%*

Austin Cox LHP

Born: 03/28/97 Age: 24 Bats: L Throws: L
Height: 6'4" Weight: 185 Origin: Round 5, 2018 Draft (#152 overall)

YEAR	TEAM	LVL	AGE	W	L	SV	G	GS	IP	H	HR	BB/9	K/9	K	GB%	BABIP
2018	BUR	ROK	21	1	1	0	9	9	33^1	29	1	4.0	13.8	51	42.1%	.373
2019	LEX	LO-A	22	5	3	0	13	13	75^1	59	5	2.6	9.2	77	39.8%	.262
2019	WIL	HI-A	22	3	3	0	11	10	55^1	53	6	2.6	8.5	52	32.5%	.322
2021 FS	*KC*	*MLB*	*24*	*2*	*3*	*0*	*57*	*0*	*50*	*47*	*7*	*4.6*	*8.2*	*45*	*35.3%*	*.284*

Comparables: Nick Margevicius, David Peterson, Julio Urías

Cox doesn't have the prospect juice of his starting pitching peers in the Royals organization, but he does pique some interest. His breaking pitches—a pair of curveballs with different breaks along with a hard slider—allow him to get by in the low 90s with his fastball. He lacks the pedigree and draft status of the Fab Four from the Royals' 2018 draft, but his command of those pitches—along with a stellar work ethic—has him knocking on the door to The Show.

YEAR	TEAM	LVL	AGE	WHIP	ERA	DRA-	WARP	MPH	FB%	WHF	CSP
2018	BUR	ROK	21	1.32	3.78						
2019	LEX	LO-A	22	1.08	2.75	79	1.2				
2019	WIL	HI-A	22	1.25	2.77	107	-0.2				
2021 FS	*KC*	*MLB*	*24*	*1.46*	*4.76*	*109*	*0.0*				

Wade Davis RHP

Born: 09/07/85 Age: 35 Bats: R Throws: R
Height: 6'5" Weight: 225 Origin: Round 3, 2004 Draft (#75 overall)

YEAR	TEAM	LVL	AGE	W	L	SV	G	GS	IP	H	HR	BB/9	K/9	K	GB%	BABIP
2018	COL	MLB	32	3	6	43	69	0	65^1	43	8	3.6	10.7	78	41.3%	.238
2019	COL	MLB	33	1	6	15	50	0	42^2	51	7	6.1	8.9	42	39.8%	.349
2020	COL	MLB	34	0	1	2	5	0	4^1	9	3	6.2	6.2	3	42.1%	.375
2021 FS	KC	MLB	35	2	3	0	57	0	50	47	7	5.3	8.8	48	40.0%	.290

Comparables: Arthur Rhodes, Steve Cishek, Jim Gott

That might be all they wrote for Davis' multifaceted career. A ballooned ERA and evaporating velo, coupled with a shoulder injury, led to an abrupt adieu with Colorado, who knocked him off the roster in the final week of this silly season. We may see a return in some capacity—he was replaced as closer by Daniel Bard, after all—but if that was the final chapter, let us remember Davis as a middling Rays starter who turned into the Trojan workhorse in Now That's What I Call A Wil Myers Trade Vol. 1. Or as the lockdown setup man for baseball's unlikely Brigadoon, the World Series-bound Royals, allowing one run in 25 of their postseason innings. And possibly, we can remember him for that one moderately neato Cubs season. But as they have written about Mike Hampton, let us forget he ever pitched for the Rockies.

YEAR	TEAM	LVL	AGE	WHIP	ERA	DRA-	WARP	MPH	FB%	WHF	CSP
2018	COL	MLB	32	1.06	4.13	87	0.8	95.6	49.1%	29.7%	
2019	COL	MLB	33	1.88	8.65	129	-0.4	95.1	46.2%	25.1%	
2020	COL	MLB	34	2.77	20.77	136	0.0	93.4	40.3%	19.6%	
2021 FS	KC	MLB	35	1.52	5.03	107	0.0	95.1	46.6%	26.1%	40.7%

Foster Griffin LHP

Born: 07/27/95   Age: 25   Bats: R   Throws: L
Height: 6'3"   Weight: 225   Origin: Round 1, 2014 Draft (#28 overall)

YEAR	TEAM	LVL	AGE	W	L	SV	G	GS	IP	H	HR	BB/9	K/9	K	GB%	BABIP
2018	NWA	AA	22	10	12	0	28	26	152^2	197	20	2.4	6.9	117	37.4%	.360
2019	OMA	AAA	23	8	6	0	25	25	130^2	134	20	4.4	7.6	111	48.9%	.295
2020	KC	MLB	24	1	0	0	1	0	1^2	0	0	0.0	5.4	1	80.0%	.000
2021 FS	KC	MLB	25	2	3	0	57	0	50	50	7	4.5	7.3	40	44.2%	.291

Comparables: Zack Littell, Sal Romano, Justus Sheffield

At a crossroads after the 2019 season, Griffin found a pitching consultant, embraced Rapsodo technology and threw 23 innings for Tigres Del Licey in the Dominican Winter League. In an age of power pitchers, the fastball isn't going to impress. But with an improved cutter, he was rewarded with a spot on the 40-man, and ultimately, a spot on the Opening Day roster. He made his major-league debut on his 25th birthday, recorded five outs ... and left the game with what was ultimately diagnosed as a torn UCL. Pitching can be such a cruel art. He will spend 2021 rehabbing from Tommy John, and with the young arms on the Royals' horizon, will face an uphill battle to get big-league innings down the road. But dammit, this story needs a better ending.

YEAR	TEAM	LVL	AGE	WHIP	ERA	DRA-	WARP	MPH	FB%	WHF	CSP
2018	NWA	AA	22	1.55	5.13	103	0.4				
2019	OMA	AAA	23	1.52	5.23	90	3.0				
2020	KC	MLB	24	0.00	0.00	103	0.0	93.8	30.4%	30.8%	
2021 FS	KC	MLB	25	1.51	4.95	112	-0.1	93.8	30.4%	30.8%	38.2%

Kansas City Royals 2021

Jackson Kowar RHP

Born: 10/04/96   Age: 24   Bats: R   Throws: R
Height: 6'5"   Weight: 180   Origin: Round 1, 2018 Draft (#33 overall)

YEAR	TEAM	LVL	AGE	W	L	SV	G	GS	IP	H	HR	BB/9	K/9	K	GB%	BABIP
2018	LEX	LO-A	21	0	1	0	9	9	26¹	19	2	4.1	7.5	22	53.4%	.239
2019	WIL	HI-A	22	5	3	0	13	13	74	68	4	2.7	8.0	66	44.9%	.305
2019	NWA	AA	22	2	7	0	13	13	74¹	73	8	2.5	9.4	78	45.5%	.323
2021 FS	KC	MLB	24	2	3	0	57	0	50	47	7	4.2	7.8	43	42.5%	.284
2021 DC	KC	MLB	24	0	0	0	3	3	14.3	13	2	4.2	7.8	12	42.5%	.284

Comparables: Robert Dugger, Jorge Alcala, Anthony Misiewicz

   Who doesn't love a list? When the Royals popped five collegiate pitchers with their first five picks of the 2018 draft, it was irresistible to rank them in some sort of category. Upside? Closest to majors? Floor? Set 'em up and rank 'em! With a fastball/change combo, Kowar was probably the least sexy of the five and would generally rank toward the bottom of such lists after the draft. (That's not a criticism … the Royals selected some exciting, electric arms.) But since then he's added some velocity to the heater, bringing it up to the mid-90s while maintaining a change that can fade and dive. All he's missing is a quality breaking pitch to make the upside really jump. Still, he projects to the rotation, which might be why the Royals ranked him second among the five.

YEAR	TEAM	LVL	AGE	WHIP	ERA	DRA-	WARP	MPH	FB%	WHF	CSP
2018	LEX	LO-A	21	1.18	3.42	80	0.4				
2019	WIL	HI-A	22	1.22	3.53	97	0.3				
2019	NWA	AA	22	1.26	3.51	96	0.3				
2021 FS	KC	MLB	24	1.42	4.63	109	0.0				
2021 DC	KC	MLB	24	1.42	4.63	109	0.1				

Asa Lacy LHP
Born: 06/02/99   Age: 22   Bats: L   Throws: L
Height: 6'4"   Weight: 215   Origin: Round 1, 2020 Draft (#4 overall)

Perhaps it's true and there's no such thing as a pitching prospect. But damn if the Royals aren't trying to figure it out. Lacy, the fourth-overall selection in the 2020 draft out of Texas A&M, joins the stable of collegiate arms the club has drafted the last couple of years. Since arriving on campus three years prior, he added muscle to an athletic frame and started hitting the mid-90s with the heat. While that's tantalizing to be sure, it's the slider, with nasty horizontal break coming out of the same slot as the fastball, that makes scouts swoon. Ever see an actual scout swoon? Strikeout 46 batters in 24 innings with a four-pitch mix and you need to order a round of smelling salts. Kansas City has been aggressive with their young college arms, moving them quickly through the system, so it will be interesting to see where they start the right-hander after an abbreviated collegiate season and a summer of inter-squad matchups.

Richard Lovelady LHP
Born: 07/07/95   Age: 26   Bats: L   Throws: L
Height: 6'0"   Weight: 185   Origin: Round 10, 2016 Draft (#313 overall)

YEAR	TEAM	LVL	AGE	W	L	SV	G	GS	IP	H	HR	BB/9	K/9	K	GB%	BABIP
2018	OMA	AAA	22	3	3	9	46	0	73	53	3	2.6	8.8	71	49.5%	.266
2019	OMA	AAA	23	1	2	4	24	0	26¹	26	1	2.4	9.9	29	52.7%	.357
2019	KC	MLB	23	0	3	0	25	0	20	30	2	3.6	7.7	17	50.0%	.418
2020	KC	MLB	24	0	0	0	1	0	1	1	1	9.0	0.0	0	33.3%	.000
2021 FS	KC	MLB	25	2	2	0	57	0	50	47	5	3.1	8.6	47	48.3%	.294
2021 DC	KC	MLB	25	2	2	0	57	0	61	57	7	3.1	8.6	58	48.3%	.294

Comparables: José Quijada, Tanner Scott, Nestor Cortes

When your name is literally "Dick Lovelady," your options for future employment are fairly limited. You *could* be the inspiration for a series of romance novels best read quickly and discreetly and on the beach. You could become the Used Car Sales director of the fourth-most prosperous Chevy dealership in your Tri-State area. Or you could emerge as a major-league reliever who conspicuously leads the league in shirsey sales. Our protagonist doesn't miss enough bats or retire enough righties to walk through door no. 3, but there's huge demand for used cars right now.

Kansas City Royals 2021

YEAR	TEAM	LVL	AGE	WHIP	ERA	DRA-	WARP	MPH	FB%	WHF	CSP
2018	OMA	AAA	22	1.01	2.47	55	2.1				
2019	OMA	AAA	23	1.25	3.08	38	1.1				
2019	KC	MLB	23	1.90	7.65	115	-0.1	95.6	60.8%	17.7%	
2020	KC	MLB	24	2.00	9.00	153	0.0	93.0	53.8%	0.0%	
2021 FS	KC	MLB	25	1.29	3.85	93	0.4	95.5	60.5%	16.8%	51.9%
2021 DC	KC	MLB	25	1.29	3.85	93	0.5	95.5	60.5%	16.8%	51.9%

Daniel Lynch   LHP

Born: 11/17/96   Age: 24   Bats: L   Throws: L
Height: 6'6"   Weight: 190   Origin: Round 1, 2018 Draft (#34 overall)

YEAR	TEAM	LVL	AGE	W	L	SV	G	GS	IP	H	HR	BB/9	K/9	K	GB%	BABIP
2018	BUR	ROK	21	0	0	0	3	3	11^1	9	0	1.6	11.1	14	55.2%	.310
2018	LEX	LO-A	21	5	1	0	9	9	40	35	1	1.4	10.6	47	48.0%	.351
2019	ROY	ROK	22	0	0	0	3	3	9	6	0	3.0	12.0	12	55.6%	.333
2019	BUR	ROK+	22	1	0	0	2	2	9	13	1	3.0	7.0	7	55.2%	.429
2019	WIL	HI-A	22	5	2	0	15	15	78^1	76	4	2.6	8.8	77	46.9%	.324
2021 FS	KC	MLB	24	2	2	0	57	0	50	46	6	3.5	8.3	45	45.8%	.282

Comparables: Julio Urías, Albert Abreu, Tarik Skubal

It's about *The Stuff*. And Lynch has it in spades. A fastball that tickles 99 mph with life, a slider that has plus-potential and an above-average change … Yeah, that's *The Stuff* alright. The next step was to harness that into a repeatable, smooth delivery that maintains a center of balance and sync. He reported to the alternate camp site in the summer and remained in Kansas City for an extended camp following the end of the season in hopes of making up for lost minor-league innings. There he continued to refine those mechanics while toying with an improved changeup. Even though a couple of his comrades in arms accelerated their timetable and debuted in the majors in 2020, he remains the starting pitching prospect with the highest upside.

YEAR	TEAM	LVL	AGE	WHIP	ERA	DRA-	WARP	MPH	FB%	WHF	CSP
2018	BUR	ROK	21	0.97	1.59						
2018	LEX	LO-A	21	1.02	1.57	83	0.6				
2019	ROY	ROK	22	1.00	1.00						
2019	BUR	ROK+	22	1.78	4.00						
2019	WIL	HI-A	22	1.26	3.10	91	0.5				
2021 FS	KC	MLB	24	1.31	3.96	93	0.4				

Royals Prospects

The State of the System:
This looked like a system on the rise last year. Some of that was interrupted by a lost minor league season, but a strong draft helped out.

The Top Ten:

1 ★ ★ ★ *2021 Top 101 Prospect* **#9** ★ ★ ★

Bobby Witt Jr.   **SS**   OFP: 70   ETA: 2022
Born: 06/14/00   Age: 21   Bats: R   Throws: R   Height: 6'1"   Weight: 190
Origin: Round 1, 2019 Draft (#2 overall)

The Report: Witt was in contention to go 1.1 in the 2019 draft, and the tools at the time were loud enough to carry the mantle of "first-overall prep shortstop." The athletic tools both grade out at 6 or better, and he had the infield actions to project at shortstop long term. The raw power was plus, with potential projection beyond that if he filled out more physically. The one place you could quibble with the profile was exactly how much he would hit. Projecting the hit tool for any prep bat is going to be an exercise in high variance, but even a fringe hit tool with swing-and-miss issues—a below median, but not unreasonable projection on draft day—would be enough given the rest of the skill set. A couple steps past that though, and Witt might be a superstar.

Development Track: Witt jumped from the AZL to the alternate site where he faced a fair amount of major-league-quality arms. He showed improving contact ability and a real two-strike approach, which portend the kind of hit tool improvements that would really make the offensive profile pop. The raw power has started to translate into (simulated) games as well, and he could be a 25-plus home run bat at his peak. He has seen some time at third base as well. That might be a better fit for him if he fills out more and has a clearer path to the majors in Kansas City at the moment. Witt is clearly trending up despite not having a real minor league season, and he was already quite a good prospect this time last year.

Variance: High. My initial instinct here was to put medium, but despite the positive alternate site reports and the strong tools across the board, Witt hasn't seen real game time outside of the complex, where he slugged .354. So we will remain somewhat cautious.

Mark Barry's Fantasy Take: In this Golden Age of Fantasy Shortstops, Witt's potential pilgrimage to the hot corner doesn't affect his fantasy value all that much. He's a top-20ish dynasty name with or without shortstop eligibility. The steals will be the deciding factor for his fantasy ceiling. If he runs consistently, we're looking at a potential top-five prospect, and a guy who could see plenty of time in the first three rounds of standard roto drafts.

───── ★ ★ ★ *2021 Top 101 Prospect* **#21** ★ ★ ★ ─────

2 Asa Lacy   LHP   OFP: 60   ETA: Late 2022/Early 2023
Born: 06/02/99   Age: 22   Bats: L   Throws: L   Height: 6'4"   Weight: 215
Origin: Round 1, 2020 Draft (#4 overall)

The Report: There was little question of who was the best pitching prospect entering the draft, with Lacy setting himself above the rest of a strong group of college arms. Surprisingly, he wasn't the first pitcher taken and fell into the Royals' laps at the fourth pick. Lacy's combination of physical build and an advanced four-pitch mix allow us to project him as a frontline starter, with far less reliever risk than most pitching prospects. While the mechanics could be classified by some as "funky," he repeats the delivery well and does a very good job of hiding the ball before release. It helps an already plus fastball in the mid-to-upper 90s jump on hitters and shorten the reaction time available on anything breaking or off-speed.

Development Track: The shortened college season may have helped Lacy where it hurt others. Many players needed the season to showcase and improve their skills, whereas in limited innings, Lacy not only was able to demonstrate his abilities, but also kept close to 100 innings off his arm without any risk of overuse. Being prepped and ready to go for a full season in 2021 is all that is required at present.

Variance: Medium. Pitchers are always a fickle bunch to forecast. There seems to be a low risk he won't pan out as a starter, and it's not out of the realm of outcomes he turns into an ace.

Mark Barry's Fantasy Take: Lacy was my favorite pitcher in the 2020 draft by far, and was probably closer to my favorite player in the draft than was appropriate. I'm not sure what more you could ask for than a lefty with four pitches who can flirt with high-90s heat. It's hard to bet on pitching prospects in dynasty leagues, so when you do, make sure there's ace upside. Lacy has ace upside, and is probably one of my five favorite pitching prospects in baseball.

───── ★ ★ ★ *2021 Top 101 Prospect* **#70** ★ ★ ★ ─────

3 Daniel Lynch   LHP   OFP: 60   ETA: Late 2021/Early 2022
Born: 11/17/96   Age: 24   Bats: L   Throws: L   Height: 6'6"   Weight: 190
Origin: Round 1, 2018 Draft (#34 overall)

The Report: Lynch's fastball jumped shortly after being drafted and it's been all systems go for his prospect track since. It's mid-90s heat from the left side with two potential above-average secondaries in his slider and change. The slider was ahead when he was last pitching in minor league games, although both secondaries needed more refinement and consistency. Even with the potential for a robust three-pitch mix, Lynch's mechanics have always suggested reliever, and he missed some time in 2019 with an arm injury.

Development Track: Lynch continued pumping his 70 fastball down the road at the alternate site at T-Bones Stadium. The changeup was his main developmental focus and he's made strides with the pitch. There have been general command improvements as well. The last hurdle for him is to throw 100+ innings in the upper minors, but if those go as well as his low minors outings, his last few 2021 appearances could be in the majors.

Variance: Medium. A lefty who can run it up into the upper 90s will get major league chances if he can stay healthy. There are also good second and third options in the arsenal. The profile and injury risks are not insignificant, though.

Mark Barry's Fantasy Take: No shade at Lynch—he's a backend, top-100 guy—but my excitement in this system really drops off after the top two dudes. I think there's a very strong chance Lynch is a reliever, so he's less interesting in a fantasy sense. There's upside to dream on, but I'm not terribly confident he gets there.

───── ★ ★ ★ *2021 Top 101 Prospect* **#95** ★ ★ ★ ─────

4 Jackson Kowar   RHP   OFP: 60   ETA: 2021
Born: 10/04/96   Age: 24   Bats: R   Throws: R   Height: 6'5"   Weight: 180
Origin: Round 1, 2018 Draft (#33 overall)

The Report: Another in the long line of high-pick pitchers to come out of Kevin O'Sullivan's Florida program, Kowar featured an unusually good changeup for a college pitcher and it's been his out pitch as a pro as well. It plays well off his mid-90s fastball although the command, although his mechanics have never screamed sure-shot starter, and the curve has been fringy. He's pitched well in the minors, but hasn't dominated quite as much as you'd expect from a major college arm with a plus fastball/change combo. That's left him in the kind of mid-rotation starter or late-inning reliever prospect who is on the outside of our Top 101 zone rather than in the 80-100 range somewhere. That's not a large distinction in projection, to be fair.

Development Track: Kowar continued to get his velocity back at the alternate site, getting up to 99 while sitting comfortably in the mid-90s. The curve has reportedly improved enough to be an average offering, and that's all he will really need given the fastball and change. You'd like to see the command get to the happy side of average to feel a bit more confident about his having immediate success, but he's basically major-league ready, and will likely make the cut for the 101 this time around.

Variance: Medium. The breaking ball is good enough now that he's less likely to end up as a fastball/change reliever, and the changeup might be good enough that he ends up the Chris Paddack who was promised. He's probably just a third starter though. And that's fine.

Mark Barry's Fantasy Take: Kowar strikes guys out, but doesn't post gaudy numbers. He has solid rates, but they're not spectacular. He's got a Backend Starter, uh, starter's kit, which is certainly useful irl but less so in fantasy circles.

─────── ★ ★ ★ *2021 Top 101 Prospect* **#97** ★ ★ ★ ───────

5 **Erick Pena** **CF** OFP: 60 ETA: 2024/2025
Born: 02/20/03 Age: 18 Bats: L Throws: R Height: 6'3" Weight: 180
Origin: International Free Agent, 2019

The Report: Shortly after signing, we started hearing that Peña was clearly the second best prospect of his IFA class, behind only Jasson Dominguez. While Dominguez looks likes a middle linebacker who hits dingers, Peña is your typical toolsy, projectable center field prospect with a present swing to make scouts blush. There's always going to be a fairly high level of uncertainty with a 17-year-old outfielder, and that was certainly true of Peña at this time last year. He was high potential, but needed to add strength and professional experience.

Development Track: Despite not having games in which to to play, Peña was invited to postseason camp at Kauffman and instructs. Sending him up to face the likes of Lynch and Kowar was a big ask, and he was overmatched early on, but adjusted to the level of competition and then shined at instructs against more age-appropriate pitching. Peña has added some good weight already and should continue to fill out and turn his present doubles power into plus over-the-fence game power in his 20s. He remains a potential five-tool center fielder, and we're more bullish on that this year than last.

Variance: Extreme. This cuts both ways. He has very little professional experience and won't turn 18 until spring training. But I've suspected for a bit that he's eventually going to grow into an elite outfield prospect, and nothing I've heard this year has dissuaded me of that possibility.

Mark Barry's Fantasy Take: Last year in this space, I wrote that Peña could be a decent fallback in FYPDs if you missed out on Jasson Dominguez. Since, Peña has surged up prospect boards despite literally not playing in a real game. The lesson, as always, is these J2 guys come with helium. You need to get in early if you're getting in at all. I'd have Peña in the top-75 or so, but even that is all on speculation at this point.

6. Kyle Isbel OF   OFP: 55   ETA: Mid-to-late-2021
Born: 03/03/97   Age: 24   Bats: L   Throws: R   Height: 5'11"   Weight: 183
Origin: Round 3, 2018 Draft (#94 overall)

The Report: Isbel was aggressively assigned to High-A Wilmington to start his first full campaign in 2019, and shined there until he broke his hamate and missed several months. When he came back, he struggled badly in one of MiLB's worst hitting environments, tanking his offensive numbers for the season. Despite the low average, he projects as an above-average hitter with strong feel for contact. He has a good plate approach and pitch recognition and sneaky power, especially to the pull side. He's also a plus runner and fielder. Basically, if the average is what we think it could be, and not what it was in 2019, he's going to be a solid regular with a broad base of offensive and defensive abilities.

Development Track: Along with Witt, Isbel was one of Kansas City's top performers at the alternate site, continuing his strong run from the 2019 Arizona Fall League. We said last year that we wanted to see him pull everything together for a full season, and that holds true. He has not even moved up in the rankings here given the strong nature of the system overall. But make no mistake, his stock is decently up year-over-year.

Variance: Medium. We're still missing the single big season, but he's done everything other than that now.

Mark Barry's Fantasy Take: I think Isbel is a little under-the-radar on the dynasty scene. As Jarrett mentioned, his hit tool projects as above average and the 23-year-old has displayed some efficiency on the bases. There's 20/20 potential for Isbel, and I don't think you'd have to pay that price on the current market.

7. Nick Loftin   OFP: 55   ETA: Late 2022 or early 2023
Born: 09/25/98   Age: 22   Bats: R   Throws: R   Height: 6'1"   Weight: 185
Origin: Round CBA, 2020 Draft (#32 overall)

The Report: Loftin was one of the names that was floated around a bunch of different landing spots on draft night. There isn't one particularly loud tool that stands out, which perhaps limits his overall ceiling. However, his at least average grades across the board and positional versatility creates a relatively high floor. Loftin has a balanced swing that creates a ton of contact to all fields and some pull-side pop.

Development Track: Even with the possibility of playing multiple spots on the diamond, he's more than capable of handling short. The swing and the approach are tied together so any adjustments made will affect the other side of the equation. It would be wise to get him situated his first full year, with any alterations offensively or defensively coming later. He could be a quick mover who ascends alongside the others on this list as the next wave makes their way to Kansas City.

Variance: Low. The difference between his likely outcome and worst case scenario as a valued bench player isn't all that much. He's a big league asset one way or another.

Mark Barry's Fantasy Take: The deeper the league, the more interest I'd have in a guy like Loftin. Adding a guy who can play a few different spots and won't kill you anywhere offensively is a nice luxury, but the lack of impact anywhere keeps me from endorsing him in any format shallower than 15 teams.

8. Khalil Lee CF   OFP: 55   ETA: 2021
Born: 06/26/98   Age: 23   Bats: L   Throws: L   Height: 5'10"   Weight: 170
Origin: Round 3, 2016 Draft (#103 overall)

The Report: Lee has long been a bit of a prospect enigma. He has big bat speed and plus raw power, but hasn't really gotten to it since he was in Low-A in 2017. His groundball rates spiked absolutely huge once he was promoted to Double-A; 59 percent over the late stage of 2018 and 2019 combined. Throw in some serious swing-and-miss—his swing gets long and out of sync, which contributes to both issues—and we've been concerned about Lee's long-term offensive trajectory for a while. He does run like the wind and can play anywhere in the outfield, and even moderate swing adjustments could get him on the fast track.

Development Track: Lee was a part of the summer camp and alternate site group all season. The Royals believe he made some of the adjustments to make better and more contact there, and added him to the 40-man roster after the season.

Variance: High. We're going to need to see his adjustments in games—and make sure that they don't cause his hit tool to cave in—before we truly believe in it.

Mark Barry's Fantasy Take: Lee stole 53 bases in 2019. That's it. That's the reason we're clinging to hope in a fantasy sense. It's also the reason we'll keep clinging to that hope, probably against our collective better judgment.

9. MJ Melendez C   OFP: 55   ETA: 2022/2023
Born: 11/29/98   Age: 22   Bats: L   Throws: R   Height: 6'1"   Weight: 185
Origin: Round 2, 2017 Draft (#52 overall)

The Report: As you can see in his statistics box, Melendez absolutely *cratered* in 2019 in Wilmington. It was a complete collapse of his hit tool; his timing fell apart and he didn't make enough contact or hit it in good spots when he did. Yet you only need to run it back another year to see a potential star catcher. Melendez was our No. 67 overall prospect entering the 2019 season, with huge raw power and big defensive talents. If his hit tool can even get to below-average, he'll be a pretty good regular, and if it can get past that he'll be a star. But it's pretty hard to stay afloat hitting .163.

Development Track: Melendez was at the alternate site all season, gaining valuable experience and reps. He impressed early on, though he wore down over the course of training. He's still a year away from being added to the 40-man, and we'd like to see a consolidation season here.

Variance: Extreme. There's severe hit tool variance here, both to push him above the OFP and to implode his entire offensive skill set a la 2019.

Mark Barry's Fantasy Take: I'm working on a theory that catching prospects are a little like Highlanders in that there can be only one. Right now it's Adley Rutschman, and pretty much everyone else is off my radar. Also Melendez struck out almost 40 percent of the time during his last bout with competitive pitching, so he'll need to iron out those issues before getting back into the mix.

10   Carlos Hernández   RHP   OFP: 50   ETA: Debuted in 2020

Born: 03/11/97   Age: 24   Bats: R   Throws: R   Height: 6'4"   Weight: 250
Origin: International Free Agent, 2016

The Report: An over-aged signee out of Venezuela in 2016, Hernandez found mid-90s heat as a late-bloomer. He's pitched well in the minors, but his large frame hasn't proved as durable as you'd like, and there's some effort in the delivery. The profile might play better in relief, but he does have feel for both a change and curve, although the change can be a bit firm and flat, and the 12-6 curve lacking tight, late depth.

Development Track: Despite not pitching above the South Atlantic League, Hernandez was called up as an available arm on the 40-man roster, and briefly slotted into the Royals' rotation in place of Matt Harvey. The results were mixed at best. He touched the upper-90s with regularity and both the curve and change flashed above-average, but when they weren't flashing, they got hit hard, and the fastball command was well-below-average. Hernandez has the potential to have big, bat-missing stuff, but he looked like a pitcher who needed another year-plus in the minors to harness it all.

Variance: Medium. I'm fairly confident Hernandez would be a useful reliever, if the arsenal doesn't end up deep enough, or the durability issues continue. But he's not a major-league ready reliever, and there's limited upside as a rotation piece.

Mark Barry's Fantasy Take: Hernandez wasn't great in his first stint with the big club, being used as an opener in three of his five appearances. I'm not sure you need to spend a ton of time contemplating his fantasy future, but if you want to do so as an attempt to take your mind off of the world's insanity, I won't begrudge you.

The Prospects You Meet Outside The Top Ten

#11

Nick Pratto 1B Born: 10/06/98 Age: 22 Bats: L Throws: L Height: 6'1" Weight: 195 Origin: Round 1, 2017 Draft (#14 overall)

Pratto has been disappointing as a prospect, given he was a first-round prep bat, and his 2019 at Wilmington was an out-and-out disaster, even factoring in how hard it is to hit there. But he also got one of the strongest positive reports among prospects at the alternate site. The swing has improved, and if he can get more aggressive with his approach in the zone, a potential average regular is back in play.

Prospects to dream on a little

Wilmin Candelario SS Born: 09/11/01 Age: 19 Bats: S Throws: R Height: 5'11" Weight: 165 Origin: International Free Agent, 2018

Signed for $850,000 out of the Dominican as part of Kansas City's 2018 J2 class, Candelario needs to add some physical strength to up the oomph in his natural hitting ability, but could be year or two away from being a very intriguing two-way shortstop prospect.

Darryl Collins OF Born: 09/16/01 Age: 19 Bats: L Throws: R Height: 6'2" Weight: 185 Origin: International Free Agent, 2018

Signed out of the Dutch League, Collins found himself back with the Curaçao Neptunus in 2020 before heading back for instructs. His is a frame that portends power although the approach at the plate is still raw and he can't consistently lift and pull the ball at present. There's some feel for contact already, so he may be able to unlock some poolside power at some point, but he'll have to hit a bunch as the arm will limit him to left field.

Rothaikeg Seijas RF Born: 07/22/02 Age: 18 Bats: R Throws: R Height: 5'11" Weight: 170 Origin: International Free Agent, 2018

Seijas was reputed to be the best pure hitter of the recent Kansas City IFA classes, but he is on the shorter and already-filled-out side. There's some power potential here, but he may end up as more of a tweener, which does feel like an unnecessarily specific thing to write about an 18-year-old who hasn't even come stateside yet.

You always need catching

Sebastian Rivero C Born: 11/16/98 Age: 22 Bats: R Throws: R Height: 6'1" Weight: 195 Origin: International Free Agent, 2015

Rivero is a career .250/.291/.345 hitter in the minors. Even considering he's a catcher, he would have to be a really good glove to be much more than a fringe backup. But the defensive improvements this year do give him a really good glove. And as the sign says, you always need catching.

Good upside but a ways away

Zach Haake RHP Born: 10/08/96 Age: 24 Bats: R Throws: R Height: 6'4" Weight: 186 Origin: Round 6, 2018 Draft (#182 overall)

We had very strong 2019 reports on Haake, who flashed three above-average or plus pitches as a breakout arm who thrived in the pros after struggling at Kentucky. If the season had happened, he might've broken out even further; instead, he ended up a bit behind due to shoulder soreness (which also cost him some time in 2019) and never made it to the alternate site. He's healthy now, but he's entering his age-24 season having never pitched above Low-A and there's durability and secondary consistency issues present. It sure feels like there's a lot of bullpen risk, in other words.

You were going to ask about him in the comments

Seuly Matias   RF   Born: 09/04/98   Age: 22   Bats: R   Throws: R   Height: 6'3"   Weight: 198   Origin: International Free Agent, 2015

Matias is now over three years removed from his breakout in the Appy, and two years removed from hitting 31 home runs in just over 90 games in the South Atlantic League. The hit tool completely collapsed in 2019. The swing-and-miss that was always a concern has borne out, so while the line-to-line power is elite, it seems unlikely Matias will get it into games against advanced arms. There were some marginal approach gains at the alternate site, but the profile is trending more towards "wins a lot of Double-A Home Run Derbies" than "major league masher." It's a shame, because it's a really fun batting practice.

Top Talents 25 and Under (as of 4/1/2021):

1. Bobby Witt Jr., SS
2. Brady Singer, RHP
3. Adalberto Mondesi, SS
4. Asa Lacy, LHP
5. Kris Bubic, LHP
6. Daniel Lynch, LHP
7. Jackson Kowar, RHP
8. Erick Pena, OF
9. Brad Keller, RHP
10. Kyle Isbel, OF

Brady Singer stepped into the major-league rotation a bit ahead of schedule. He was immediately a good No. 3 starter, which was exactly our projection for him on last year's prospect list. He's mostly a sinker/slider guy, with the occasional changeup mixed in. Both of his primary offerings are effective, and although he's never going to miss a ton of bats and doesn't have elite upside, the whole is greater than the sum of the individual parts due to pitchability and command. We expect him to continue on at this level for quite some time.

Adalberto Mondesi makes his last 25U list this year. He remains a frustrating offensive player, unable to get on base enough to take advantage of his blazing speed or to leverage his power. He's put up two terrible offensive seasons in a row, 75 DRC+ in 2019 and 61 in 2020, and Witt is starting to loom as a long-term threat to his job. There's still a chance this all comes together, but he might just stay a speed-and-defense type, too.

Kris Bubic made it even more ahead of schedule than Singer, having jumped straight from High-A to The Show. He was slightly-above replacement level by DRA, though with a shinier 4.32 ERA and striking out nearly a batter an inning. He gave up a few too many walks and dingers, but for that big of a jump it didn't go that badly. He works mostly off his fastball and changeup, with a curve that's a better third offering than most of the type. Like Singer, he projects to be a mid-rotation starter, but unlike Singer he's not actually there quite yet.

Brad Keller is one of the better recent Rule 5 finds. That's not saying that much, since he's only a fourth starter-type, but getting a fourth starter for free is always a plus. Edward Olivares, our No. 14 prospect in a loaded Padres system last year, landed here in the Trevor Rosenthal trade, and warrants a brief mention as well; he graduated on service time without establishing himself as a regular, but we think he's got a shot to get there.

Part 3: Featured Articles

Royals All-Time Top 10 Players

by Rob Mains

POSITION PLAYERS

SALVADOR PÉREZ, C (2011–Present)
Catching is a tough position. Between 2013 and 2018, only three American League catchers qualified for the batting title (502 plate appearances) more than once. Stephen Vogt and Russell Martin did it twice. Pérez did it five times, and fell 3 plate appearances short of a sixth. He also won Gold Gloves in five of those seasons. Due to his impatience at the plate has to keep his power production and batting average up to be an offensive positive, and he's constantly dinged for poor pitch-framing, but somehow the full package works. After missing 2019 with Tommy John surgery, he returned to post a career-best .986 OPS. He's not done climbing up this list.

MIKE SWEENEY, 1B/DH (1995–2007)
He played on some dreadful Royals teams (the team had one winning season in his 13 years) and was usually its prime source of power, batting third or fourth and hitting .299/.369/.492. He has the second-most homers, 197, in franchise history. His 144 RBI in 2000 remains the most ever by a Royal.

FRANK WHITE, 2B (1973–1990)
The outstanding product of the Royals' baseball academy, White was quietly outstanding throughout an 18-year career, all with the Royals. He won eight Gold Gloves. Early in his career, he didn't hit much but was a good basestealer, swiping 114 bags from 1975 to 1980. Later, he developed pop, hitting 78 homers from 1984 to 1988. Second only to Brett in games played as a Royal, his name was on the lineup card in at least 75 percent of Royals games for fourteen straight seasons. He's ninth all-time with 2,151 games at the keystone.

GEORGE BRETT, 3B (1973–1993)

For a long time, the greatest third baseman in AL history was…Eddie Mathews? Brooks Robinson? Home Run Baker? Then Mike Schmidt debuted in 1972, Brett in 1973, and we all forgot about the old-timers. Thirteen-time All-Star, received MVP votes in 11 years (won it in 1980, when he hit .390, highest in the league since Ted Williams' .406 in 1941), Brett could do it all. He hit 40-plus doubles in a season five times, 10 or more triples four times, 20-plus homers 10 times. He was a great fielder, if not in the same class as Brooks Robinson and Graig Nettles, and hit .337/.397/.627 in 43 postseason games (his homer off Goose Gossage in the 1980 ALCS may be the most famous hit in franchise history).

AMOS OTIS, OF (1970–1983)

The trade that brought Otis to Kansas City from the Mets in exchange for Joe Foy is one of the most lopsided in major league history. Foy played 140 games for the Mets and Senators while Otis. anchored center field in Kansas City for 14 years, batting .280/.347/.433 with 193 homers, 341 stolen bases, and three Gold Gloves. His one-handed catches in the outfield won over Royals fans and he and pitcher Steve Busby were the first players inducted into the team's Hall of Fame.

WILLIE WILSON, OF (1976–1990)

Wilson joined the Royals in 1978, when Otis was ensconced in center field, so he began is career as a left fielder, moving to center after Otis was traded after the 1983 season. He's remembered primarily for his speed. His 612 stolen bases are by far the team record, and he had only four fewer triples than Brett despite playing in a third fewer games. He holds the team single-record of 230 hits in 1980, when he scored 133 runs and stole 79 bases. Led the league in three-baggers five times and hit .305 over his first seven seasons. A change in hitting style greatly reduced his effectiveness thereafter.

CARLOS BELTRAN, OF (1998–2004)

He played only five full seasons in Kansas City and was hurt for part of one of them. In the other four, he drove in and scored 100-plus runs every year, batting .287/.352/.483. With free agency looming, the Royals traded him in 2004 and he went on to post above-average batting numbers with six other clubs.

ALEX GORDON, OF (2007–2020)

He started his career at third base but moved to left field in 2010 and won eight Gold Gloves there. He was a slightly above-average hitter over his career but in his prime, from 2011 to 2015, he drove the ball into the gap (leading the league with 51 doubles in 2012) and got on base consistently (.359 OBP), becoming a reliable run-producer at the top of the lineup.

LORENZO CAIN, OF (2011-2019)

The Royals have sure had a run of center fielders. He came to the club from Milwaukee in the Zack Greinke deal and was the team's regular center fielder from 2013 through 2017. Like his predecessors, he was an outstanding fielder, winning a Fielding Bible Award in 2014. He was MVP of the 2014 ALCS, when he hit .533/.588/.667 and made two sensational catches against Baltimore. He hit .289 for the Royals, stole 120 bases, and was the no. 3 hitter for the 2015 World Champions.

HAL McRAE, DH (1973-1987)

The well-respected slugger came to Kansas City via a lopsided trade with the Reds and was a devastating hitter (.293/.356/.458) for the team. He played primarily right field his first year with the team but became its primary designated hitter for the rest of his career. He was known for his aggressive running; google "Hal McRae slide" for a primer on slides into second that are no longer allowed.

PITCHERS

PAUL SPLITTORFF, LHP (1970-1984)

The franchise leader in starts, innings, wins, and losses, Splittorff started 296 games between 1972 and 1980, second-most in the league. He was the starting pitcher for the franchise's first game at Kauffman Stadium (originally Royals Stadium) in 1973. He was known for a high leg kick and was the definition of a "crafty lefty," relying on guile rather than velocity.

DENNIS LEONARD, RHP (1974-1983, 1985-1986)

From 1975 to 1981, no right-handed pitcher won more games than Leonard, the only pitcher to throw 200 innings every year during the span. He won 20 or more games three times and is the franchise leader in complete games (103) and shutouts (13). His 3.70 ERA—all with the club—is fourth among Royals pitchers with at least 100 starts. Pitcher workloads were out of control in the 1970s and Leonard suffered for it after averaging 273 innings and 16 complete games a season from 1976-1980. He was also one of a handful of pitchers (and one of just here non-knuckleballers) to start 40 games in a season after the early 1970s. He ultimately broke down via a knee injury but repetitive stress damage can show up anywhere, not just the arm.

LARRY GURA, LHP (1976-1985)

He came to the Royals by way of a trade from the Yankees for catcher Fran Healy, who played only 74 games in pinstripes. After two years in the bullpen, he switched to the rotation and was tied for second in the American League with 186 starts from 1978 to 1983. He was the best pitcher on the playoff teams of 1978, 1980 and 1981. His .587 wining percentage (111-78) is the highest among Royals pitches with at least 1,100 innings. A pitch-to-contact lefty, Gura's career strikeout rate of 3.5 per nine is the fourth-lowest among the 47 pitchers to throw at least 2000 innings during his career.

DAN QUISENBERRRY, RHP (1979–1988)

The submariner led the American League in saves five times, threw 120 or innings in relief five times, and had a sparkling 2.55 ERA over 573 games in Kansas City. A smart and funny man, he was exceptionally popular with both teammates and fans. When the Royals were invited to the White House after winning the 1985 World Series, President Reagan apologized to Quisenberry for calling him "Jim" in a call to the clubhouse after the seventh game. Quisenberry replied, "That's OK, Don." Career unintentional walk rate was 0.79 per nine.

CHARLIE LEIBRANDT, LHP (1984–1989)

Leibrandt came to Kansas City after spending six years in the Reds organization. He carried a career 4.42 ERA in 315.2 innings when he swapped red for powder blue (in return for fringe reliever Bob Tufts). The change of scenery worked. After posting a 7-1 record and 1.24 ERA in nine starts at Triple-A Omaha, Leibrandt, at 27, joined the Royals' rotation and ranks third in starts, innings, and wins among Kansas City lefties with a 3.60 ERA. Traded to the Braves after an off-year; between the two teams he was somehow 1-7 in postseason play despite a 3.77 ERA.

BRET SABERHAGEN, RHP (1984–1991)

Before we better understood pitcher arm injuries, Saberhagen averaged 234 innings per season over five years before his 26th birthday (and over 162 innings in a season only three times after). That total included arguably the best pitching year in team history, 1989, when he led the league with a 23-6 record, 2.16 ERA, and 12 complete games. He won the Cy Young Award that year and in 1985, when he was World Series MVP, allowing only one run in two complete-game wins over the Cardinals. The former 19th-round draft pick had first-round control, walking just 1.8 batters per nine during his Royals career.

MARK GUBICZA, RHP (1984–1996)

A steady performer who pitched all but two of his career games for Kansas City, Gubicza ranks second in franchise history in starts, innings, and strikeouts. After averaging over 31 starts per year in his first six seasons, Gubicza suffered a torn rotator cuff in 1990. Often a career-ending injury, he came back to pitch six more years in Kansas City, remarkably leading the league with 33 starts in 1995.

JEFF MONTGOMERY, RHP (1988–1999)

Like McRae and Leibrandt, he came via a terrible trade for the Reds (the Royals gave up outfield prospect Van Snider). Montgomery was Quisenberry's successor as the Royals' when McRae became the Royals' manager during the 1991 season. Unlike his predecessor, Montgomery's arsenal prioritized the hard stuff, but, unusually for a closer, he had a complete assortment of breaking balls to offer as well. Holds the team record with 304 saves and 686 appearances. His 45 saves in 1993 tied Quisenberry's 1983 team record (since twice broken by Greg Holland).

KEVIN APPIER, RHP (1989–1999)

He played in only one All-Star game and got Cy Young Award votes in only one season, but from 1990 to 1997, Appier was probably the best pitcher in the American League after Roger Clemens. The Royals had only three wining seasons in his time in Kansas City, but his fastball-slider-forkball combination flummoxed hitter during the high-offense Nineties. His 1,458 strikeouts are a team record and his 3.49 ERA was the best in team history relative to the league average.

ZACK GREINKE, RHP (2004–2010)

If there's an argument as to whether Saberhagen's 1989 season was the best in team history, it's posed by Greinke's 2009, when he was 16-8 with a 2.16 ERA, striking out over a batter an inning and winning the Cy Young Award. Another star traded away before he hit free agency, his surface numbers—60-67 record, 3.82 ERA—are belied by the high-offense era in which he pitched (his park- and era-adjusted career ERA trails only Appier and Saberhagen) and the poor Royals teams for which he pitched.

A Taxonomy of 2020 Abnormalities

by Rob Mains

I'm going to start this with a trivia question. Trust me, it's relevant. Don't bother skipping to the end of the article to find the answer, it's not there.

Only five players have appeared in 140 or more games for 16 straight seasons. Who are they?

It's a trivia question starting off an essay, so you know how this works: Whatever you guessed, you're wrong. It's okay. As someone who purchased this book, chances are good that you're an educated baseball fan. But the circumstances behind 2020 force us to abandon, or at least seriously question, some of our favorite patterns and crutches for evaluating the game we love.

We just completed what was undoubtedly the strangest season in MLB history. No fans, geographically limited schedule, universal DH, seven-inning twin bills, runners on second in extra innings, a 16-team postseason, a club playing at a Triple-A stadium. Some of these changes will likely persist (sorry), but we've never had so many tweaks dumped on us all at once, at least not since they figured out how many balls were in a walk.

And the biggest, of course, was the 60-game season. The 19th century was dotted with teams that went bankrupt before the season ended, but the lone season with only 60 scheduled games was 1877. That year there were only six teams, the league rostered a total of 77 players (just 16 more than the 2020 Marlins), and batters called for pitches to be thrown high or low by the pitcher, who was 50 feet away. We can say the 2020 season was easily the shortest ever for recognizable baseball.

As such, it'll stand out. Few abbreviated seasons do. Just about everybody reading this knows the 1994 season ended after Seattle's Randy Johnson struck out Oakland's Ernie Young for the last out of the Mariners-A's game on August 11. The ensuing player strike wiped out the rest of the season and the postseason. Teams played only 112-117 games that year.

And many of you know that a strike in the middle of the 1981 season split the season in two, resulting in the only Division Series until 1995. Teams played only 103-111 games that year, the shortest regular season since 1885.

Those two seasons are memorable. So when we see that nobody drove in 100 runs in 1981, or that Greg Maddux was the only pitcher with 180 or more innings pitched in 1994, we think, "Of course. Strike year."

But we don't remember other short years. You might not recall that the 1994 strike spilled into the next year, chopping 18 games off the 1995 schedule. You might've read that the 1918 season, played during the last pandemic, ended after Labor Day due to the government's World War I "work or fight" order. A strike erased the first week and a half of the 1972 season, but that year's best known as the last time pitchers batted in the American League.

The point is, while we don't remember small changes to the schedule, we remember the big ones. The 1981 mid-season strike. The 1994 season- and Series-ending strike. And, of course, the pandemic-shortened 2020 season. We won't need a reminder why Marcell Ozuna's 18 homers were the fewest to lead the National League in a century. (Literally; Cy Williams led with 15 in 1920.)

Now, about that trivia question. The five players are Hank Aaron, Brooks Robinson, Pete Rose, Ichiro Suzuki, and Johnny Damon. The one nobody gets, of course, is Damon, and a lot of people miss Ichiro, whose last season of 140-plus games came garbed in the red-orange and ocean blue of Miami when he was 42. That's half of what makes it a good question. The other half is the two guys whom many think made the list but didn't. Lou Gehrig? His streak started in the Yankees' 42nd game of the 1925 season and lasted only 13 seasons after that. And everybody assumes Cal Ripken Jr. did it, having played 2,632 straight games over 17 seasons. But one of those 17 seasons was 1994, when the Orioles played only 112 games.

My point? *I just told you* everybody remembers the 1994 strike year, but everybody forgets it fell in the middle of Ripken's streak, separating the first twelve years from the last four. Just because we recall something doesn't mean it's always at the front of our minds.

Nobody is going to forget 2020, and baseball is obviously not the main reason. But there will come a time in the future when you're looking at a player's or a team's record, and there will be baffling numbers there for 2020, and you'll think, "I wonder what happened." (Not to mention the missing line for minor league players.) Just like you forgot that the 1994 strike limited Ripken to 112 games.

Try not to forget it, though. The 2020 season resulted in weird statistical results for several reasons.

There were only 60 games.

I know, duh. But that had impacts beyond counting stats like Ozuna's home run total or Yu Darvish and Shane Bieber leading the majors with eight wins. (I know, pitcher wins, but still.)

The 162-game season is the longest among major North American sports, and that duration gives us a gift. Over the course of a long season, small variations tend to even out. A player who has a ten-game hot streak will probably have a ten-game cold streak. A team that starts the year losing a bunch of close games will probably win a bunch of them. We get regression to the mean. Statistics stabilize.

Consider flipping a coin. Over the long run, we expect it to come up heads about half the time. But the fewer flips, the more variation there'll be. If you flip a coin six times, probability theory tells us you'll get at least two-third heads about 34 percent of the time. Flip it 30 times, your chance of two-thirds heads drops to five percent.

Or, relevant to this case, if you flip a coin 60 times, your chance of getting at least 36 heads—that's 60 percent—is 7.75 percent. Expand the coin-flipping to 162 times, and the chance of getting 60 percent heads drops to 0.73 percent.

In other words, the odds of an outcome that's 20 percent better (or worse) than expected is *more than ten times higher* when you flip your coin 60 times than when you do it 162 times. Call it small sample size, call lack of mean reversion, or call it luck not evening out, 162 is a lot more predictive than 60. You get much more variation over 60 games than over 162. Bieber's 1.63 ERA and 0.87 FIP aren't something we'd see over a full season, and neither is Javier Baéz's .203/.238/.360.

Some players' lines in 2020 look normal. Brian Anderson had an .811 OPS in 2019 and an .810 OPS in 2020. (He probably would have gotten that last point if he'd been given enough time.) But there are many like Bieber and Baéz, some of them from young players still establishing their talent levels. The answer to the question, "What went right or wrong for that guy in 2020?" is most likely "Nothing, it was just a 2020 thing."

Preseason training was abbreviated for hitters.

Every year, spring training drags. Players get tired of it, fans get tired of it, and you sure can tell sportswriters get tired of it. Yes, something to get everyone into shape is necessary, but does it really have to drag on for over a month? Can't we shorten it?

The 2020 season answered in the negative, at least for hitters. Warren Spahn is credited with saying that hitting is timing and pitching is upsetting timing. It appears nobody had his timing down after the abbreviated July summer camp. Through August 9—18 games into the season—MLB batters were hitting .230/.311/.395 with a .275 BABIP. That BABIP, had it held, would have been the lowest since 1968, the Year of the Pitcher. In recent years it's hovered around .300.

It didn't hold. Play returned to more normal levels the rest of the year: .249/.325/.425 with a .297 BABIP starting August 10. But batters whose play concentrated in those first two weeks wound up with ugly lines. Andrew

Benintendi went on the injured list with a season-ending rib cage strain on August 11. His final line: .103/.314/.128 in 14 games. Franchy Cordero went on the IL with a hamate bone fracture on August 9 and a .154/.185/.231 line. Even though he came back strong in a late September return, it was too late to repair his full-season numbers.

Preseason training was abbreviated for pitchers.

Every year, spring training drags. Players get tired of it, fans get tired of it … wait, I already said that. But the abbreviated preseason was tough on pitchers, too. As noted, they had the upper hand coming out of the gate. But then they lost that hand. And then their arms, too.

The 2020 season was spread over 67 days. During those 67 days, 237 pitchers hit the Injured List, compared to 135 in the first 67 days of 2019. A lot of those IL stints, though, were COVID-19-related. Still, over the first 67 days of the 2019 season, there were 72 pitchers on the IL with arm injuries. That figure jumped to 110 in 2020, a 53 percent increase.

There are a number of factors contributing to pitcher arm injuries, ranging from usage to velocity, but it appears that attenuated preseason training played a role. A lot of pitchers had super-short seasons due to arm woes. Corey Kluber, Roberto Osuna, and Shohei Ohtani combined for seven innings, none after August 8. All suffered arm injuries. We'll never know whether they'd have fared better with a longer preseason, but we can guess how they probably feel.

Everybody played.

Rosters were set to expand from 25 to 26 in 2020, so even if we'd had a normal season, we'd have likely seen 2019's record of 1,410 players on MLB rosters broken. But due to the pandemic, rosters started the year at 30 and were cut to only 28. Add multiple COVID-19 absences and the revolving door caused by poor starts by hitters and a rash of pitcher arm injuries, and 1,289 players appeared in MLB games in 2020. The comparable figure over the first 67 days of the 2019 season was 1,109. That 16 percent increase works out to an average of six more players per team in 2020 compared to a similar slice of 2019. A future look back at 2020 rosters will include a lot of unfamiliar names.

Plus became a minus.

In advanced metrics, we adjust batter and pitcher performance for park and league/era variations. A plus sign appended to the end of a measure means that it's adjusted for park and league. It's scaled to an average of 100, with higher figures above average and lower figures below average. (Similarly, a metric with a minus is also park- and league-adjusted and scaled to 100, with lower values better.) Here at BP, our advanced measure of offensive performance is DRC+. Baseball-Reference has OPS+ and FanGraphs has wRC+.

Using park and league adjustments, we can compare Dante Bichette's 1995 Steroid Era season at pre-humidor Coors Field (.340/.364/.620, 40 homers, 128 RBI, MVP runner-up) with Jim Wynn's 1968 Year of the Pitcher season at the cavernous Astrodome (.269/.376/.474, 26 homers, 67 RBI, no MVP votes). It's not close. DRC+, OPS+, and wRC+ all give the nod to Wynn, handily. This is a useful tool. As my Baseball Prospectus colleague Patrick Dubuque tweeted last fall, "Please note that when I ask how you are, I am already adjusting for era."

The 2020 season messes up plus (and minus) stats for two reasons. First, the park adjustment was based on only 30 home games instead of the usual 81. Everything noted above regarding the short season applies, literally doubly, to park effect calculations. DRC+ uses a single-season park factor. OPS+ uses a three-year average and wRC+ five years. The figure for 2020 is suspect.

Second, OPS+ and wRC+ adjust for league: American and National. (DRC+ adjusts for opponent, regardless of league.) While there were two leagues in 2020, they were an artificial construct. To reduce travel, teams played opponents geographically, not based on league. There weren't two leagues, American and National. There were three, Western, Central, and Eastern.

That makes a difference because teams in the same league played in different run-scoring environments. AL teams scored 4.58 runs per game, NL teams 4.71. That's a small difference. But teams in the East scored 0.21 more runs per game (4.95) than teams in the West (4.74), and they both scored a lot more than Central teams (4.25). Adjusting for league misses that difference, so this book will be safe in that regard, but other sources may be distorted somewhat.

Not every game was a "game."
In 2020, the rising tide of strikeouts was finally stemmed. Strikeouts per team per game fell from 8.8 in 2019 to 8.7 in 2020. That marked the first decline after 14 straight annual increases.

In 2020, the rising tide of strikeouts rose higher. Batters struck out in 23.4 percent of plate appearances compared to 23.0 percent in 2019. That marked the 15th straight annual increase.

Both are true statements.

Because of two rule changes—seven-inning doubleheaders and runners on second in extra innings—games in 2020 were unprecedented in their brevity. There were 37.0 plate appearances per game in 2020. The only years with fewer were 1904 and 1906-1909. The average game in 2020 entailed 8.61 innings pitched, the fewest since 1899.

So when you see any per-game stats for 2020, you need to increase them by 3 or 4 percent to get them on equal footing with recent years.

Kansas City Royals 2021

Or, better, just ignore them. Last year happened. There were major league games contested between major league teams. But when you're looking at those physical or electronic baseball cards, when you're weaving narratives over why this young player's inevitable rise to stardom fell apart or why that old veteran rekindled his magic, don't linger on the 2020 line. It was just too weird.

Thanks to Lucas Apostoleris for research assistance.

—Rob Mains is an author of Baseball Prospectus.

Tranches of WAR

by Russell A. Carleton

We ask "replacement level" to be a lot of things. Sometimes contradictory things. Sometimes I wonder if we know what it even means anymore. The original idea was that it represented the level of production that a team could expect to get from "freely available talent", including bench players, minor leaguers, and waiver wire pickups. It created a common benchmark to compare everyone to, and for that reason, it represented an advancement well beyond what was available at the time. In fact, it created a language and a framework for evaluating players that was not just better but *entirely* different than what came before it.

But then we started mumbling in that language. The idea behind "wins above replacement" was one part sci-fi episode and one part mathematical exercise. Imagine that a player had disappeared before the season and suddenly, in an alternate timeline, his team would have had to replace him. The distance between him and that replacement line was his value. We need to talk about that alternate timeline.

Without getting too into 2:00 am "deep conversations" with extensive navel-gazing, it's worth thinking about why one player might not be playing, while another might.

- A player might not be playing because he has a short-term injury or his manager believes that he needs a day off.
- A player might not be playing because he has a longer-term injury that requires him to be on the injured list.

There's a difference here between these two situations. In particular, the first one generally *doesn't* involve a compensatory roster move, while the second one does. It's possible, though not guaranteed, that the person who will be replacing the injured/resting player would be the same in either case. That matters. Teams generally carry a spare part for all eight position players on the diamond, although in the era of a four-player bench, those spare parts usually are the backup plan for more than one spot.

Kansas City Royals 2021

A couple of years ago, I posed a hypothetical question. Suppose that a team had two players in its system fighting for a fourth outfielder spot. One of them was a league average hitter, but would be worth 20 runs below average if allowed to play center field for a full season. One of them was a perfectly average fielder, but would be 15 runs below average as a hitter, if allowed to play an entire season. Which of the two should the team roster? It's tempting to say the second one, as overall, he is the better player. That misses the point. A league average hitter on the bench isn't just a potential replacement for an injured outfielder. He might also pinch hit for the light-hitting shortstop in a key spot. You keep the average hitter on the roster, even though he isn't a hand-in-glove fit for one specific place on the field, because being a bench player is a different job description than being a long-term fill-in for someone. If you find yourself in need of a longer-term fill-in, you can bring the other guy up from AAA.

When we're determining the value of an everyday player though, if he had disappeared before the season and a team would have had to replace his production, they likely would have done it with a player who was a long-term fill-in type because they would have had to replace a guy who played everyday. Maybe that's the same guy that they would have rostered on their bench anyway, but we don't know. It gets to the query of what we hope to accomplish with WAR. Are we looking for an accurate modeling of reality or are we looking for a common baseline to compare everyone to? Both have their uses, but they are somewhat different questions.

Let's talk about another dichotomy.

- A player might not be playing because he isn't very good and is a bench-level player.
- A player might not be playing because there is another player on the team who has a situational advantage that makes him the better choice today. The classic case of this is a handedness platoon. On another day, he might be a better choice.

When we think about player usage, I think we're still stuck in the model that there are starters and there are scrubs. We have plenty of words for bench players or reserves or backups or utility guys. We do still have the word "platoon" in our collective vocabulary, but in the age of short benches, it's hard to construct one. It's always been hard to construct them. You have to find two players who hit with different hands, have skill sets that complement each other, and probably play the same position. In the era of the short bench, one of them had probably better double as a utility player in some way. Baseball has a two-tiered language geared toward the idea of regulars and reserves. The fact that it was so easy for me to find plenty of synonyms for "a player whose primary function is to come into a game to replace a regular player if he is injured or resting" should tell you something.

I'm always one to look for "unspoken words" in baseball. What is it called when someone is both half of a platoon and the utility infielder? That guy exists sometimes, but he reveals himself in that role—usually by accident. We don't have a word for that, and whenever I find myself saying "we don't have a word for that", I look for new opportunities. What do you call it, further, when the job of being the utility infielder is decentralized across the whole infield with occasional contributions from the left fielder? It's not even a "super-utility" player. What happens when you build your entire roster around the idea that everyone will be expected to be a triple major?

⚾   ⚾   ⚾

I think someone else beat me to this one, and on a grand scale. Platoons work because we know that hitters of the opposite hand to the pitcher get better results than hitters of the same hand, usually to the tune of about 20 points of OBP. If you want to express that in runs, it usually comes out to somewhere around 10 to 12 runs of linear weights value prorated across 650 PA. But hang on a second, now let's say that we have two players who might start today, both of roughly equal merit with the bat. One has a handedness advantage, but is the worse fielder of the two. In that case, as long as his "over the course of a season" projection as a fielder at whatever position you want to slot him into is less than a 10-run drop from the guy he might replace, then he's a better option today.

We're not used to thinking of utility players as bat-first options, who would play below-average defense at three different infield positions. That guy might hook on as a 2B/3B/LF type (Howie Kendrick, come on down!) but teams usually think to themselves that they need as their utility infielder someone who "can handle" shortstop, the toughest of the infield spots to play. If someone can do that *and* hit well, he's probably already starting somewhere, so he's not available as a utility infielder. It's easier for those glove guys to find a job. In a world where the replacement for a shortstop *has to be* the designated utility infielder, that makes sense.

But as we talked about last week, we're living in a different world. The rate at which a replacement for a regular starter turns out to be *another starter* shifting over to cover has gone way up over the last five years. There was always some of it in the game, but this has been a supernova of switcheroos. Now if your second baseman is capable of playing a decent shortstop, that 2B/3B/LF guy can swap in. He's not actually playing shortstop, and maybe the defense suffers from the switch, but if he's got enough of a bat, he might outhit those extra fielding miscues. And in doing so, he is effectively your backup shortstop.

Somewhere along the lines, teams got hip to the idea of multi-positional play from their regulars. I've written before about how you can't just put a player, however athletic, into a new position and expect much at first. The data tell us that. Eventually, players can learn to be multi-positionalists, but it takes time, roughly on the order of two months, before they're OK. But there's a hidden message in there. If you give a player some reps at a new spot, he's a reasonably gifted athlete and somewhat smart and willing to learn, he could probably pick it up enough to get to "good enough," and it doesn't take forever. You just have to be purposeful about it. Maybe you get to the point where you can start to say "he's still below average but we could move him there and get another bat into the lineup, and it's a net win."

Teams have started to build those extra lessons into their player development program. It used to be seen as a mark of weakness to be relegated to "utility player" because that meant that you were a bench player (all those synonyms above come with a side of stigma). Now, it's a way of building a team. If you get a few reps in the minors (where it doesn't count) at a spot, you'll have at least played the spot at game speed before. There are limits to how far you can push that. A slow-footed "he's out in left field because we don't have the DH" guy is never going to play short, but maybe your third baseman can try second base and not look like a total moose out there.

⚾   ⚾   ⚾

Back to WAR. I'd argue that the world of starters and scrubs is slowly disintegrating, for good cause. In the event that a regular starter really does go down with an injury–ostensibly, the alternate universe scenario that WAR is attempting to model–it makes the team a little more resilient to replacing him. And the good news is that you're more likely to be able to replace him with the best of the bench bunch, rather than the third-best guy, because the best guy doesn't have to be an exact positional match for the guy who got hurt. And that's what the manager would want to do. He'd want to replace that long-term production, not with an amalgam of everyone else who played that position, but with the best guy available from his reserves.

Now this is still WAR. We still want to retain the principle that we should be measuring a player, and not his teammates. We need some sort of common baseline, and despite what I just said, we'll still need some sort of amalgam. To construct that, I give to you the idea of the tranche. The word, if you've not heard it before, refers to a piece of a whole that is somehow segmented off. It's often used in finance to talk about layers of a financial instrument.

Here, I want you to consider that there are 30 starters at each of the seven non-battery positions (catchers should have their own WAR, since only a catcher can replace a catcher). We can identify them by playing time, and we can futz around with the definition a little bit if we need to. Next, among those who aren't in that starting pool, we identify the top tranche of the 30 best bench players, which I would again identify by playing time, and then the second and third and fourth and so on. If a player were to disappear, his manager would probably want to take a guy from that top tranche of the bench to replace him. In a world where even the starters can slide around the field, that becomes more feasible.

We can take a look at that top tranche and say "How many of them showed that they are able to play (first, second, etc.)?" and therefore could have directly substituted for the starter? How many of them could have been a direct substitute for our injured player? We don't know whether one of them would be on *a specific* team, but we can say that 40 percent of the time, a manager would have been able to draw from tranche 1 in filling the role, and 35 percent from tranche 2. But on tranche 1, we can also look at how many of those players played a position that could have then shifted and covered for that spot. We'd need some eligibility criteria for all of this (probably a minimum number of games played) but it would just be a matter of multiplication. Shortstop would be harder to fill, and managers would probably be dipping a little further down in the talent pool, and so replacement level would be lower, as it is now.

Doing some quick analysis, I found that the difference in just batting linear weights (haven't even gotten into running or fielding) between tranche 1 and tranche 2 in 2019 was about 6.5 runs, prorated across 650 PA. Between tranche 1 and tranche 3, it's 10.8 runs. The ability to shift those plate appearances up the ladder has some real value.

This part is important. We can also give credit to starters for the positions that they showed an ability to play, even if they didn't play them (this is the guy fully capable of playing center, but who's in a corner because the team already has a good center fielder) because he allows a team to carry a player who hits like a left fielder to functionally be the team's backup center fielder. He facilitates that movement upward among the tranches. We can start to appreciate the difference between a left fielder who would never be able to hack it in center (and the compensatory move that his team would have to make) and the left fielder who could do it, but just didn't have to very often.

Past that, you can continue to use whatever hitting and fielding and running metrics you like to determine a player's value, but when we get down to constructing that baseline, I'd argue we need a better conceptual and mathematical framework. It's going to require some more #GoryMath than we're used to, but I'd argue it's a better conceptualization of the way that MLB actually plays the game in 2020. If…y'know…MLB plays in 2020. If WAR is going to be our flagship statistic among the *acronymati*, then we need to acknowledge that it contains some old and starting-to-be-out-of-date assumptions about the game. We may need to tinker with it. Here's my idea for how.

—*Russell A. Carleton is an author of Baseball Prospectus.*

Secondhand Sport

by Patrick Dubuque

Back before time stopped, I liked to go to thrift stores. Now that I'm older, I rarely ever buy anything—I don't need much in my life, now—but I still enjoy the old familiar circuit: check to see if there are baseball cards to write about, look for board or card games to play with the kids, scan for random ironic jerseys, hit the book section. It takes ten, maybe fifteen minutes. Thrift stores are the antithesis of modern online shopping, because you don't know what they have, and you don't even really know what you want. It's junk, literal junk, stuff other people thought was worthless. That's what makes it great.

In an idealized economy, thrift stores shouldn't exist. Everybody has a living wage, and every product has a durability that exactly matches its desired life; nothing should need to be given away, no one should need to be given to. But then, thrift stores shouldn't work on a customer experience level, either. You wouldn't think an ethos of "let's make everything disorganized and hard to find" would lead to customer satisfaction, but low-budget retailers like TJ Maxx and Ross thrive on this model. People like bargain hunting as much for the hunting as the bargain; it's part of the experience, spending time as if it's a wager. There's a thrill, occasionally, in inefficiency.

In sports, the modern overuse of the word "inefficiency" is a condemnation: It insinuates that there is *an* efficiency, a correct way to be found, and that all other ways are wrong ways. It's prevalent in baseball but hardly contained to it; the lifehack, the Silicon Valley disruption are other examples of productivity creep in our daily lives. Their modern success makes plenty of sense. Maximization of resources, after all, is its own puzzle, and an industry of European board games is founded upon it. It's fun to take a system and optimize it, unravel it like a sudoku puzzle. If there's only one kind of genius, after all, there's no way anyone can fail to appreciate it.

Baseball has been hacking away at these perceived inefficiencies since its inception: platoons, bullpens, farm systems were all installed to extract more out of the tools at hand. But it's been a particular badge of the sabermetric movement, from Ken Phelps and his All-Star Team to Ricardo Rincon and the darlings of *Moneyball*. It's business, but it's also an ethos: the idea that there's treasure among the trash, something we all failed to appreciate until someone brought it to light.

It's the myth that made Sidd Finch so enticing, that fuels so many "best shape" narratives and new pitch promises. We all, athletes and unathletic sportswriters, want to believe that there's genius trapped inside us, and that it's just a matter of puzzling out the combination to unlock it. That our art, our style is the next inefficiency, waiting for our own Billy Beane. It's why we root for underdogs, and why we're excited for the Mike Tauchmans and the Eurubiel Durazos, champions of skin-deep mediocrity.

Except we aren't anymore, really. The days of "Free X" have descended beyond the ring of irony and into obscurity. There are still Xs to be freed, or at least one X, duplicated endlessly: Mike Ford, Luke Voit, Max Muncy. The undervalued one-dimensional slugger demonstrated how the game hasn't quite culturally caught up to its logical extreme. But for those who don't fit the rather spacious mold, times are grimmer. As Rob Arthur revealed several months ago, there's been a marked increase in the number of sub-replacement relievers. It's the outcome of a greater number of teams forced to play out games without the talent to win them, but it's also emblematic of the modern tendency of teams to dispose of their disposable assets, burning through cost-controlled arms the way that man chopped down forests in *The Lorax*. Stuff just isn't built to outlive their original owners anymore.

It's unsurprising, given how well-mined the market for inefficiencies has been of late. The disciples of the early analytics departments, and the disciples of those, have proliferated the league, with only a few backwater holdouts. The league has grown smarter, but every team has learned the same lesson. In fact, the phenomenon creates a peculiar kind of feedback loop: As teams value a specific subset of players or skills, prospective athletes learn to increase their own marketability by conforming themselves to the demands of their prospective employers.

And that's tragic, in the way that the extinction of animals is tragic; a certain amount of biodiversity in baseball has been lost. Shortstops hit like outfielders. Pitchers don't hit at all. Only the catchers remain idiosyncratic, thanks to the defensive demands of their position; eventually they too will be required to produce like everyone else, or they'll meet the fate of their battery mates. A perfect economy requires perfect production.

I mentioned earlier that more and more, I leave thrift stores empty-handed. It is true that I am more discerning than in the past; my bookshelves are full, and there are more streaming films than I will ever be able to watch. But there are other factors at play.

Thrift stores are, in a way, the bond markets of retail. When the economy is rough and other retailers are struggling, more people look secondhand for their products. But as recently as last year, publications were noting a reversal of the trend: Companies like Goodwill and Savers were expanding despite a strong economy. Publications credited a heightened sense of environmentalism and a rejection of cutting-edge fashion as drivers behind the increase, though the more likely answer is the modern American economy hasn't showered its favors equally, particularly among the young.

But it is more than just the economy. Baseball and thrift stores share something else in common, evident in our current conversations about re-starting the sport: They live in the gray area between public service and private enterprise. Thrift stores provide affordable necessities to lower-class citizens, and collectibles and fashion for the middle-class. Because of the success of the latter, prices have gone up across the board. Especially in terms of clothing, the middle-class flight from fashion into vintage has instead carried the aftereffects of fashion, including its costs, into a territory where people just want clothes. But there's another factor in the rise of prices, in the form of the internet.

The Goodwills of the world have grown smarter, too, employing the internet to extract full value from their detritus. Ebay, similarly, has lost much of the charm it had as a new frontier around the turn of the century. Everything has a price point now; even individual taste is no match for the algorithm, because anything rare, no matter how niche its market, is a collectible to someone.

The internet has had the same effect on thrift stores that sabermetrics has had on baseball; its equivalent to OBP was the bar scanner. As detailed in Slate, the rise of second-party stores on eBay and Amazon birthed an entire industry of used-good salespeople, armed with PDAs and scanners, buying books for three dollars to sell online for five. The author, Michael Savitz, reports earning $60,000 by working nearly 80 hours a week; he makes it clear that this is not a vocation of his choosing. It's long hours, with no real creativity or individuality, skimming the cream off of a local establishment and flipping it to someone with a little more money on the other side of the country. And once the vocation exists, the obvious question arises: why wait to put the wares out on the shelves? Why allow value to exist at all?

Nothing is ruined. Thrift stores will continue to sell polo shirts and DVDs, and baseball will continue to exist and make or lose money, depending on who you believe. But as we continue to refine our knowledge, we lose something in the conquest for efficiency, a delight born out of the unknown. The problem isn't the efficiency itself; we can't blame the booksellers, or the people sweeping freeways to collect grams of platinum from damaged catalytic converters. The problem is a system that requires this sort of profit-skimming behavior in order to feed families (or, for corporations, maximize shareholder return).

Kansas City Royals 2021

In times like these, with the 2020 season on the brink and the collective bargaining agreement close behind, it can often feel like the current situation is untenable. It can't keep going like this, even if we don't know what to do about it. But as with thrift stores, there's an equally irresistible feeling that it *has* to keep going, that it would be unimaginable to not have this broken, amazing sport. Both industries exist on an invisible foundation of friction, of chaos and unpredictability, even as both see their foundations buffed down to a perfect, untouchable polish. But if COVID-19 and its financial ramifications do, as some have suggested, make it such that the baseball that returns is fundamentally different than the baseball that came before, perhaps this is the time to lean in, and change the game even more. Fix bunting. Make defense more difficult. Create viable, alternate strategies. Add some chaos back into baseball. It's fun when no one knows quite where things are.

—Patrick Dubuque is an author of Baseball Prospectus.

Steve Dalkowski Dreaming

by Steven Goldman

We dream of being a pitcher, of starring in the major leagues. Depending on your age and your sense of historical perspective, you might imagine yourself as Walter Johnson, throwing harder than anyone else—hitting more batters than anyone else, too, but always feeling bad about it. You could picture yourself as a Tom Seaver or a David Cone, with all the stuff in the world but still being cerebral about it, thinking about so much more than burning 'em in there. There are so many models one could choose: You could be a Lefty Gomez, Jim Bouton, or Bill Lee, skilled, but not taking the whole thing too seriously, or a Lefty Grove, Bob Gibson, or Steve Carlton, powerful but treating each start like a mission to be survived instead of a game to be enjoyed.

Very few would dream of being Steve Dalkowski, the former Baltimore Orioles prospect who died of COVID-19 last week at the age of 80. Yet, there is something just as noble in Dalkowski's negative accomplishments—and accomplishments is what they are—as there is in the precision-engineered pitching of a Greg Maddux. You have to be very good to be that bad. Dalkowski had all of the stuff of the greatest pitchers but none of the command; his story is not one of failing to conquer his limitations, but striving against one of the cruelest hands that fate or genetics or personality can deal us: A desire to achieve great things which is almost but not quite matched by the ability to meet that goal.

As with Johnson, Grove, Bob Feller, and the rest of the hard-throwing pitchers who played before the advent of modern radar guns, we have to take the word of the players and coaches who saw Dalkowski pitch as to his velocity. He was a hard-drinking, maximum-effort pitcher who, if their memories are to be believed, consistently threw over 100 miles per hour. His was the Maltese Fastball, the stuff that dreams are made of. The problem is that velocity without command and control is still a good distance from utility. Dalkowski was the most effective towel you could design for a fish, the sleekest bathing suit intended to be worn by an astronaut, but that doesn't mean he wasn't beautiful: We can appreciate a journey even if it doesn't end at the intended destination.

Whether because of sloppy mechanics he couldn't calm, an inability to understand that a consistent 98 in the strike zone would likely be more effective than a consistent 110 out of it, or all that beer, Dalkowski could never make the adjustments that pitchers like Feller and Nolan Ryan made before him, possibly because he had so far to go: Feller, who never pitched in the minors, came up at 17 and spent three years walking almost seven batters per nine innings before settling in at 3.8 beginning when he was 20. Ryan started out walking over six batters per nine but gradually improved as his long career played out; for him to go from 6.2 walks per nine with the 1966 Greenville Mets to 3.7 with the 1989 Texas Rangers represents a 40 percent reduction. An equivalent improvement by Dalkowski would still have left him walking over 11 batters per nine innings.

Dalkowski was like *The Room* of pitchers, a player so bad he became good again. Cal Ripken, Sr., who both played with and managed Dalkowski, recalled in a 1979 *Sporting News* "where are they now" piece the occasion when the pitcher crossed up his catcher and his fastball, "hit the plate umpire smack in the mask. The mask broke all to pieces and the umpire wound up in the hospital for three days with a concussion. If they ever had a radar gun in those days, I'll bet Dalkowski would have been timed at 110 miles an hour."

Signed by the Orioles out of New Britain High in Connecticut in 1957, Dalkowski was sent to Kingsport in the Appalachian League, where he pitched 62 innings. He allowed only 22 hits in 62 innings, or 3.2 per nine, a number with no equivalent in major league history (though Aroldis Chapman came close in 2014), and also struck out 121 (17.6 per nine) and walked 129 (18.7). He was also charged with 39 wild pitches. That June, one of his fastballs clipped a Dodgers prospect named Bob Beavers and carried away part of his ear. "The first pitch was over the backstop, the second pitch was called a strike, I didn't think it was," Beavers said last year. "The third pitch hit me and knocked me out, so I don't remember much after that. I couldn't get in the sun for a while, and I never did play baseball again." Former minor leaguer Ron Shelton based the *Bull Durham* pitcher Nuke LaLoosh on Dalkowski. And yet, to see him as a figure of fun, an amusing loser, is to misunderstand something unique and strange.

Dalkowski kept on posting some of the strangest lines in baseball history. Pitching for the Stockton Ports of the Class C California League in 1960, he struck out 262 and walked 262 in 170 innings. Yet, he did improve, especially after pitching for Earl Weaver at Elmira in 1962. Weaver had previously had Dalkowski at Aberdeen in 1959, but wasn't ready to grapple with him then. This time he was. "I had grown more and more concerned about players with great physical abilities who could not learn to correct certain basic deficiencies no matter how much you instructed or drilled them," he related in his autobiography, *It's What You Learn After You Know It All That Counts*. He got permission from the Orioles to give all of his players the Stanford-Binet IQ test. "Dalkowski finished in the 1 percentile in his ability to understand facts. Steve, it was said to say, had the ability to do everything but learn." [sic]

IQ tests are problematic diagnostic tools, so take Weaver's estimate of Dalkowski's mental capabilities with a grain of salt. What's important is that even if he got to the right answer by way of the wrong reason, Weaver had learned something valuable. His insight was to stop asking Dalkowski to learn new pitches and just let him get by with the two that he had. Were Dalkowski a prospect today, that would have been a no-brainer: Can't develop a third pitch? The bullpen is right over there, sir. Player development wasn't like that then, but Weaver, temporarily Dalkowski's mentor, could let him work with what he had. According to Weaver, the pitcher responded: "In the final 57 innings he pitched that season Dalkowski gave up 1 earned run, struck out 110 batters, and walked only 11." It's not true—as per the *Elmira Star-Gazette*, as of late July, Dalkowski had walked 71 in 106 innings and finished with 114 in 160 innings, which means Dalkowski's control actually faded at the end of the season rather than improved—but that doesn't mean it didn't happen in some sense, just that it didn't happen that way. Again, it's the journey, not the destination, and his ERA was 3.04 so *something* had gone right.

Also along the way: The next spring, Orioles manager Billy Hitchcock was rooting for Dalkowski to make the team as a long-man—maybe Weaver had gotten through to him. There were things out of Weaver's control, like the universe's twisted sense of humor: that March, Dalkowski's elbow went "twang."

You sometimes read that it was the Orioles' insistence on Dalkowski learning the curve that did him in, but even if they hadn't learned their lesson, the injury was probably just a coincidence: Dalkowski had thrown an incredible number of pitches over the previous few years. Still, it testifies to the dangers of trying to get what you want and risking the loss of what you had. Dalkowski tried to come back, but the 110-mph stuff was gone. A pitcher with no control and no stuff is...a civilian. What followed were years of vagabond living, arrests for drunkenness. There were Alcoholics Anonymous meetings, assistance from baseball alumni associations, but none of it took. From the 1990s until the time of his passing he dwelt in an assisted living facility, suffering from alcohol-related dementia. He'd been a heavy drinker since his teenage years. As with all those pitches per game, there was a price to be paid. You make choices on the journey and some of them are irrevocable. It's like a fairy tale: "Bite of poison apple? Don't mind if I do."

In the aforementioned *Sporting News* profile, Chuck Stevens, the head of the Association of Professional Ballplayers of America, a ballplayer charity, said, "I've got nothing against drinking. I do it myself sometimes. But, I don't condone common drunkenness. We went through lots of heartache and many dollars, but Dalkowski didn't want to help himself and we weren't going to keep him drunk." The journey is *un*like a fairy tale: No one will come along and kiss it better, not if they're busy forming judgments.

In the end, we are left with a sort of philosophical chicken/egg conundrum: Is failing to meet your goals evidence of unfulfilled potential or the lack of it? Isn't what you did by definition what you were capable of doing? Or could you have broken through to something better with the right help, the right lucky break? These are unanswerable questions, and how we try to answer them may say more about us than about the people we're judging.

No pitcher ever has it easy. *All* pitchers must work hard. *All* pitchers must refine their craft. It's almost never just about *stuff*. Dalkowski dreaming is no insult to the great pitchers who made it; from Pete Alexander to Max Scherzer, they have all earned their way up. And yet, if it is true that we can only do as much as we can do, then the journey would be more of an adventure, the ultimate triumph or defeat more noble, if like Dalkowski we lacked 100 percent of the confidence, the command, the self-possession, the commitment, the resistance to making bad decisions that so many great players possess—to be gloriously human. Or, to put it more succinctly, it would be fun to be able to throw as hard as any person ever has. Even if just for a moment, and even if nothing more came of it than that, no one could say you hadn't lived life to the fullest.

—*Steven Goldman is an author of Baseball Prospectus.*

A Reward For A Functioning Society

by Cory Frontin and Craig Goldstein

On July 5, Nationals reliever Sean Doolittle said in the middle of a press conference regarding the restart of Major League Baseball and what would later be known as summer camp, "sports are like the reward of a functioning society." This sentence was amidst a much longer, thoughtful reply about the societal and health conditions under which MLB players were being brought back. It's a very similar sentiment to one Jane McManus used on April 7, when she discussed the White House's meeting with sports commissioners. She said "sports are the effect of a functioning society—not the precursor."

Both versions of the same sentiment spoke to a laudable ideal in the context of a country that was not addressing a rampaging virus, and opting instead to bring sports back for the feeling of normalcy rather than the reality of it. "Priorities," as McManus said.

On Wednesday, the NBA's Milwaukee Bucks conducted a wildcat/political strike, refusing to come out for Game 5 of their playoff series against the Orlando Magic. The Magic refused to accept the forfeit, and shortly thereafter other playoff series were threatened by player strikes. Eventually the league moved to postpone that day's games, folding to players leveraging their united power.

The backdrop against which these actions took place was the shooting by police of Jacob Blake. Blake was shot in the back seven times by police, as he attempted to get into his vehicle. He managed to survive the assault, but is paralyzed from the waist down.

⚾ ⚾ ⚾

The step taken to walk out, first by the Milwaukee Bucks, then subsequently by other NBA, WNBA, and MLB teams, was a step toward upholding the virtue of the sentiment described by McManus and Doolittle. But that sentiment does not align with the broad history of sports in this and other countries, a history that contradicts the core of the idealistic statement.

Sports have been a significant part of American society for most of its existence, expanding in importance and influence in recent years. The idea that society was functioning in a way that was worthy of the reward of sports for most of that time is laughable. Much of America is not functioning and has not functioned for Black people, full stop. The oppressed people at the center of this political act by players, specifically Black players, in concert throughout the NBA and in fits and starts throughout Major League Baseball, have not known a society that functions for them rather than *because* of them.

Politics has been part of the sports landscape since the inception of sport, but for just about as long people have bemoaned its presence. Sports are to be an escape, it is said. An escape from what, though? A functioning society?

No, the presence of sports has never signified a cultural or political system that is on the up and up. Rather, the presence of sports *reflect and reinforce the society* that produces them.

⚾ ⚾ ⚾

The Negro Leagues were born out of societal dysfunction. The need for entirely separate leagues, composed of Black and Latino players barred from the Major Leagues because of racism? That is not a functioning society, and yet there were sports.

Even the integration of players from the Negro Leagues resulted in a transfer of power and wealth from Black-owned businesses and communities and into white ones, mirroring the dysfunction that had bled into every aspect of American society at the time. Japheth Knopp noted in the Spring 2016 Baseball Research Journal:

> *The manner in which integration in baseball—and in American businesses generally—occurred was not the only model which was possible. It was likely not even the best approach available, but rather served the needs of those in already privileged positions who were able to control not only the manner in which desegregation occurred, but the public perception of it as well in order to exploit the situation for financial gain. Indeed, the very word integration may not be the most applicable in this context because what actually transpired was not so much the fair and equitable combination of two subcultures into one equal and more homogenous group, but rather the reluctant allowance—under certain preconditions—for African Americans to be assimilated into white society.*

To understand the value of a movement, though, is not to understand how it is co-opted by ownership, but to know the people it brings together and what they demand. When Jackie Robinson—the player who demarcated the inevitability of the end of the Negro leagues—attended the March on Washington for Jobs and Freedom in 1963, he did so with his family and marched alongside the people. He stood alongside hundreds of thousands to fight for their common civil and labor rights. "The moral arc of the universe is long," many freedom fighters have echoed, "but it bends towards justice." The bend, it is less frequently said, happens when a great mass of people place the moral arc of the universe on their knee and apply force, as Jackie, his family, and thousands of others did that day.

⚾ ⚾ ⚾

Of course, taking the moral arc of the universe down from the mantle and bending it is not without risk. Perhaps the outsized influence of athletes is itself a mark of a dysfunctional society, but, nonetheless, hundreds of athletes woke up on Wednesday morning with the power to bring in millions of dollars in revenues. That very power, as we would come to find out, was matched with the equal and opposite power to *not* bring those revenues. That power, in hands ranging from the Milwaukee Bucks, to Kenny Smith in the *Inside the NBA* Studio, from the unexpected ally, Josh Hader, and his largely white teammates to the notably Black Seattle Mariners, would be exercised for a single demand: the end to state violence against Black people. Not unlike the March itself, it sat at the intersection of the civil rights of Black Americans and bold labor action. The March on Washington stood in the face of a false notion of integration—against an integration of extraction but not one of equality—and proposed something different. Just the same, the acts of solidarity of August 26, 2020 will be remembered in stark defiance of MLB's BLM-branded, but ultimately empty displays on opening weekend.

Bold defiance like this can never be without risk. By choosing to exercise this power, the Milwaukee Bucks took a risk. They risked vitriol and backlash from those they disagreed with. They risked fines or seeing their contracts voided, as a walkout like this is prohibited by their CBA. They risked forfeiting a playoff game, one that, as the No. 1 seed in the playoffs, they'd worked all year to attain. They didn't know how Orlando would respond. It wasn't clear that other teams throughout the league would follow suit in solidarity. And it wasn't known the league would accept these actions and moderately co-opt them by "postponing" games that would have featured no players.

If the league reschedules the games, some of the athletes' risk—their shared sacrifice—will be diminished, in retrospect. But they did not know any of that when they took that risk. And it is often left to athletes to take these risks when others in society won't, especially those of their same socioeconomic status and levels of influence.

It is athletes, specifically BIPOC athletes, that take them, though, because they live with the risk of being something other than white in this country every day. They are no strangers to the realities of police brutality. It seems incongruous then, to say that sports are a reward for a functioning society when we rely on athletes to lead us closer to being a functioning society. Luckily, our beloved athletes, WNBA players first and foremost among them, understand what sports truly are: a pipebender for the moral arc of the universe. ■

—Craig Goldstein is editor in chief of Baseball Prospectus. Cory Frontin is an author of Baseball Prospectus.

Index of Names

Alberto, Hanser	16
Barlow, Scott	44
Benintendi, Andrew	76
Bolaños, Ronald	82
Bubic, Kris	46
Candelario, Wilmin	96
Collins, Darryl	97
Cox, Austin	83
Davis, Wade	84
Dozier, Hunter	18
Duffy, Danny	48
Fox, Lucius	77
Franco, Maikel	20
Gallagher, Cam	77
Gordon, Alex	22
Griffin, Foster	85
Haake, Zach	97
Hahn, Jesse	50
Harvey, Matt	52
Hernandez, Carlos	54, 95
Holland, Greg	56
Isbel, Kyle	78, 93
Junis, Jakob	58
Keller, Brad	60
Kennedy, Ian	62
Kowar, Jackson	86, 91
Lacy, Asa	87, 90
Lee, Khalil	94
Loftin, Nick	93
Lopez, Nicky	24
Lovelady, Richard	87
Lynch, Daniel	88, 90
Matias, Seuly	98
McBroom, Ryan	26
Melendez, MJ	94
Merrifield, Whit	28
Minor, Mike	64
Mondesi, Adalberto	30
Newberry, Jake	66
O'Hearn, Ryan	32
Olivares, Edward	34
Pena, Erick	79, 92
Perez, Salvador	36
Pratto, Nick	96
Rivero, Sebastian	97
Santana, Carlos	38
Seijas, Rothaikeg	97
Singer, Brady	68
Soler, Jorge	40
Starling, Bubba	79
Staumont, Josh	70
Taylor, Michael A.	42
Viloria, Meibrys	80
Witt Jr., Bobby	81, 89
Zimmer, Kyle	72
Zuber, Tyler	74

For the Joy of Keeping Score

THIRTY81 Project is an ongoing graphic design project focused on the ballparks of baseball. Since being established in 2013, scorecards have been a fundemantal part of the effort. Each two-page card is uniquely ballpark-centric — there are 30 variants — and designed with both beginning and veteran scorekeepers in mind. Evolving over the years with suggestions from fans, broadcasters, and official scorers, the sheets are freely available to everyone as printable letter-size PDFs at the project webshop: www.THIRTY81Project.com

Download, Print, Score, Repeat ...

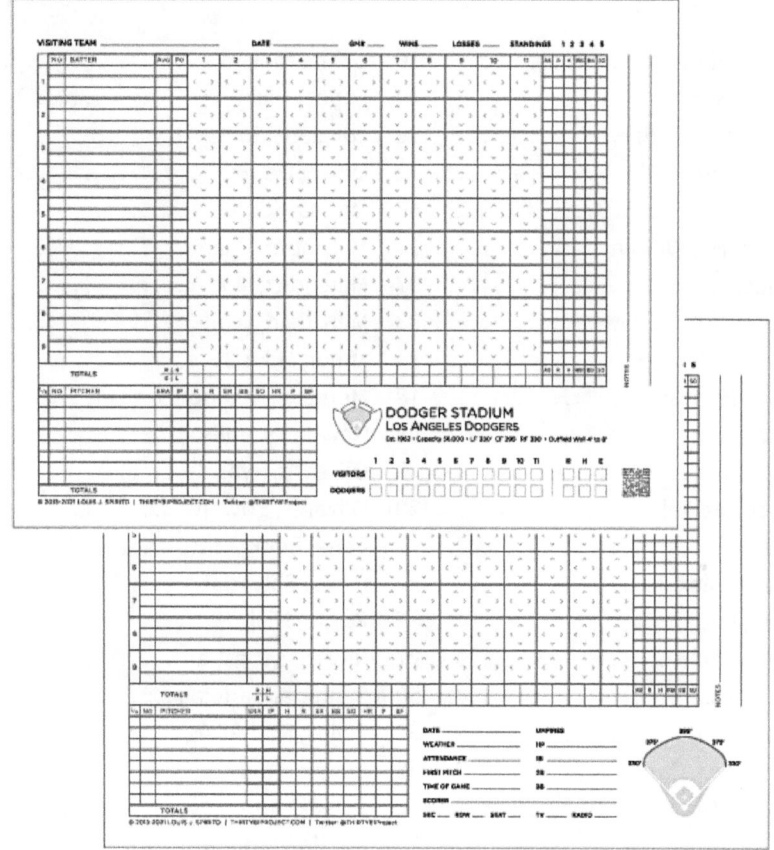